OUR MINISTERING ANGELS

A Bible Study on Angels

by Gwen R. Shaw

Engeltal Press
P.O. Box 447
Jasper, Ark. 72641
U.S.A.

Printed in the United States of America

INTRODUCTION

Are they not all ministering spirits, sent forth to minister for them who shall be heirs of salvation?'' (Hebrews 1:14)

The time has come to give the Church a frank, honest, scriptural Bible study on the topic of angels. Because of mistakes which have been made in the past, people are afraid of this subject. Yet, to be fearful of the subject of angels, because some have been led to error in the past, is as foolish as being afraid of the wind because of a tornado in Kansas, or a fire, because a neighbour's house burnt down. We must not allow our fears to rob us of the blessings which God has for us. Angels were very active all through Biblical history. The law of Moses was given by the disposition (instrumentality, arrangement) of angels. Angels attended the birth, life, resurrection and ascension of our Lord.

Angels gave John the revelation truths of the end-time. Angels will supervise the rapture and will be in charge of the outpouring of God's wrath in the days of great tribulation.

You will be blessed by this Bible study on angels and the wonderful true accounts of the ministry of angels. It is what you have been waiting for.

Gwen R. Shaw

TABLE OF CONTENTS

CHAPTER ONE

From Genesis to Revelation we can read about the activity of angels. As this age comes to a close, there will be an ever-increasing activity of angels. Angels are very important in God's economy because they are His messengers. They are always busy in their non-tiring obedience to the Heavenly Father, constantly carrying out His orders to the minutest detail.

Angels seek to explicitly obey the smallest desire and wish of their Sovereign. They know they were created to serve. They never break their ranks because they never seek to do anything which is not their purpose for existence. So, they are never jealous of other creatures, either humans or other angels like themselves. They never seek to promote themselves, nor do they bring dishonour by their conduct to their God or God's people.

Angels can be trusted to keep secrets. They only reveal that which they are permitted to reveal. When issuing commands from God or carrying out their orders, they say and do no more and no less than what is permitted them to say or do.

The reason angels are so perfect in all they do is because they are motivated by perfect love.

Jesus told us that they always "behold" the face of the Father (Matthew 18:10). That means that they come from the presence of God. This is confirmed to us by the words of the great Archangel Gabriel to John the Baptist's father Zacharias when he said, "...I am Gabriel, that stand in the presence of God;..." (Luke 1:19).

The angels know many of the great mysteries of God which we would love to know, but they are only permitted to tell that which God knows we are able to receive. It was Gabriel who explained to Mary how she would conceive the Christ child. No medical science could have explained this great mystery. Gabriel also revealed to Mary the secret of her cousin Elizabeth's pregnancy. God can trust His angels with His secrets because they do not have the human frailty of sharing gossip or speaking that which would hurt another creature. If we could ever come to the place of perfect love where our tongues would lose the power to hurt, we would certainly be more like the angels.

Angels love the unlovely. I always admire their ability to stay with a person from his birth to his death. No matter how evil that person may become, nor how many sins he may commit, the angels will never leave that person whom he is commissioned to be guardian of through all of his life's journey. It must greatly grieve an angel to see the infant, which he is in charge of, change from an innocent child into a wicked and hateful person who causes others grief and pain and even death. Perhaps the hardest thing for an angel to bear is the blasphemy and the cursing of God and His Son Jesus come from the lips of the one whom he is commissioned to stay with. The only thing that would be worse than that would be the helplessness of the angel as in death he sees the demon spirits carry that soul off to hell and know that no matter how hard he had tried to bring that soul to God and Heaven, he had failed because man is a free moral agent and has the right to choose to go to hell.

I believe every one of us has at least one guardian angel who stays with us from the time of our conception until we leave this world. I have never seen my angel, but I have felt his presence. Especially in times of danger or when I have needed God's help have been times when the angel has been very close to me.

There have, however, been times when God has shown men, by the Spirit, the presence of an angel or angels. My spirit's eyes then have seen the angel or angels, but not my natural eyes.

Angel Protects Mother

One of the times when I was permitted by the Spirit to see an angel was when I was in Germany. After my father had passed away, I was very worried about my mother living in the home without my father to protect her. There had been instances of crime and other dangerous things taking place all around the neighbourhood where she lived. While I was praying for her safety, God permitted me to see that He had stationed a big, tall angel in the hall entrance of her house who stood on guard day and night, watching over my mother back in her home in Niagara Falls, New York. I never, ever worried about her again. I knew she would always be safe in that house. Today, that house is Rainbow House; it is our missionary home.

There have been times when the Spirit of God is very powerful in our conventions that I have "seen" by the Spirit the walls of the auditorium lined with angels. During times like this the glory of God is very great.

Hallelujah Angel Tape

Angels especially love to attend meetings and gatherings where there is a great deal of high praise and true worship.

3

They have been heard to join in with the singing and the worship of the saints. Their voices are very beautiful and they can sing very high. We have the privilege of having a tape in which a vast choir of angels is heard singing. A group of young people gathered together to sing and practice some songs. As they sang, they recorded their music. Later, when they listened to the tape, they found that they not only had a recording of themselves singing, but, as they sang the eight-fold Hallelujah chorus, they were joined by a choir of thousands of voices singing much higher than is humanly possible and in addition, there were instruments heard on the tape which no one had played during the practice. We have even received letters of people being healed while listening to this tape. (See the advertisement for the "Hallelujah Angels" tape in the back of this book.) It reminded me of how, in Jesus' time, when the angel stirred the waters of the pool of Bethesda, people were also healed. (John 5:1-4)

It is strange that the tape recorder could record that which the human ear had not heard. It was only later when they listened to the tape, that they realized that angels had been singing with them.

Camera Takes Pictures of Angels

This is also true about the camera. The camera can take pictures of that which the human eye cannot see. I remember seeing a picture of a tiny cherub angel many years ago when I lived on Vancouver Island. I was pastoring a small church on Cordova Bay which was attended by a godly old couple by the name of Brice. They had moved to the island after retirement from Mr. Brice's work in Winnipeg, Manitoba. They had lost their one and only child, Dorothy, who had

4

been a very gifted singer. Dorothy had often sung solos in the large Pentecostal Assemblies of Canada church in Winnipeg. One day, after washing her hair, she and her friend went out into the garden with her small box camera to take pictures. The next day she was sick, and a few days later she died. In those days they did not have penicillin and other drugs to fight infections which could kill in days and even hours.

The parents were grief-stricken. Mr. Brice was an elder in the church, but still they could hardly be comforted. The following Sunday, as he was serving the Holy Communion in the church, he looked up and saw his dead daughter, Dorothy, smiling happily and pointing. Brother Brice looked to where she was pointing and lo and behold, there stood Jesus! She was telling her beloved, grief-stricken father, "Look to Jesus!" Though she could not speak to him, she conveyed this message.

One day, some time later, the parents remembered the camera and carefully removing the film, they took it to be developed. Imagine their surprise when they found a beautiful picture of their daughter, standing in the garden with her long hair lying over her left shoulder and just over her right shoulder the form of a beautiful cherub angel with wings! They had enlargements made and gave one of them to their friend, the famous evangelist Charles E. Price who kept it on the wall of his office while the other one hung in their own bedroom. Sister Brice showed me the picture. I was always sorry I did not get a copy also. Although Dr. Price and Brother and Sister Brice have long since gone to be with the Lord, I still can remember the sweet face of that little baby cherub. Sister Brice told me that the discovery of this photo, with its contents, gave them great comfort. She added that her daughter, Dorothy, had had a great love for babies and small children and that they felt she was ministering in Heaven to the children and infants.

Daddy Brooks

In 1972, I spent some days in Zion, Illinois, at a rest home. I needed to get away from my work to pray and fast. During my visit, I met a godly lady, Ruth Brooks. She told me about her saintly father Elder Brooks. When he was in his seventies, he was exhausted with overwork in the ministry. He had worked hard for the Lord and he felt that the Lord would soon "take him home." One day, as he was sitting on the veranda of his home, their dear friend Martha Wing Robinson walked by. She suddenly stopped and made this startling statement, "Daddy Brooks, you can choose to go home to be with the Lord now or you and Sister Brooks can leave and go for a long rest of a couple of years and then come back and serve Him for many years more."

He was surprised, as he had really felt his work was all finished. After talking it over and praying about it, he and his wife decided to take a vacation. They went to live in a cottage by the sea. For two years they rested and enjoyed walks along the seashore. Then, when he felt restored to health, they returned to Zion where he again became active and served God for about another 20 years. The Lord took him home when he was 92 years old. At his funeral the church was crowded with many friends. Unsaved photographers came to take pictures of the services. When the pictures were developed, they found that all the pictures of the coffin at the front of the church had angels flying over the coffin. Ruth gave me one of the pictures. The outline of the wings with their feather-like structure is very plainly visible. It is wonderful to know that even as angels attend the birthing of a soul, they are there to comfort the loved ones when life is over and the saint is safely going home to the Father's house.

STUDY QUESTIONS

1. What makes the angels perfect?

2. Have you had an experience with angels or do you know someone else who has had one?

CHAPTER TWO

THE ORIGIN OF ANGELS

Good and Evil Angels

God's Word is our source of information. The Bible tells us that there are both good angels and evil angels. The evil angels are those who rebelled with Lucifer and were cast out of Heaven with him. *"And there was war in heaven: Michael and his angels fought against the dragon; and the dragon fought and his angels, And prevailed not; neither was their place found any more in heaven. And the great dragon was cast out, that old serpent, called the Devil, and Satan, which deceiveth the whole world: he was cast out into the earth, and his angels were cast out with him."* (Revelation 12:7-9) This is the final victory over Lucifer and his angels who left their original state as Jude tells us in Jude 6, *"And the angels which kept not their first estate, but left their own habitation, he hath reserved in everlasting chains under darkness unto the judgment of the great day."*

One third of the heavenly hosts were cast out of their original habitation. *"And his tail drew the third part of the stars of heaven, and did cast them to the earth:..."* (Revelation 12:4) The red dragon, who is Satan and Lucifer, drew the third part of the stars (angels) of Heaven, and did cast them out. Jude tells us that these fallen angels are reserved in everlasting chains under darkness. A terrible darkness has fallen over their minds and their understanding. This is the way Satan had power to deceive them and anyone whom he

9

leads astray from God and His will. Darkness begins in the mind. When Satan can deceive a person, he has power to turn him against the truth and the righteousness of God. Pride caused Satan to fall and it has caused many people to fall. Satan wanted to be greater than God. He plotted to overthrow God and rule His angelic hosts, but God cast him out. *"How art thou fallen from heaven, O Lucifer, son of the morning! how art thou cut down to the ground, which didst weaken the nations! For thou hast said in thine heart, I will ascend into heaven, I will exalt my throne above the stars of God: I will sit also upon the mount of the congregation, in the sides of the north: I will ascend above the heights of the clouds; I will be like the Most High."* (Isaiah 14:12-14)

Lucifer Was an Angel Prince

Lucifer, which means "Morning Star" was very beautiful before his fall. He had not only great beauty, he also had great power, which God had given him. Ezekiel 28:12 describes him as being perfection personified, *"full of wisdom and perfect in beauty."* He not only was the anointed cherub that rested over the throne of God, he also had a very active part in the creation of the earth and a high position of rulership over it. Jesus called him the *"prince of this world"* (John 14:30).

Many believe he was the worship and praise leader in Heaven. He was the master musician. We certainly know that after the fall of men, it was his followers, the sons of Cain, who were the first to invent musical instruments on earth (Genesis 4:21).

Ezekiel says of him, *"Thou wast perfect in thy ways from the day that thou wast created, till iniquity was found in thee."* (Ezekiel 28:15)

Satan still has the power to put this great beauty on display at times, in order to deceive mankind.

He does this by appearing as an angel of light. *"...Satan himself is transformed into an angel of light."* (II Corinthians 11:14) This word "transformed" is *metaschematizo* which means a change of appearance rather than essence. Satan has the power to appear in many different forms, not only as an angel of light. (All good angels are angels of light, Satan only takes on the appearance of an angel of light.) He also appears in any way that is convenient for him to deceive and work a work of destruction. In the Garden of Eden, he appeared as a serpent. Sadhu Sundar Singh describes how Satan appeared to him as a very beautiful person.

Sadhu Sundar Singh's Experience

Once on a dark night I went alone into the forest to pray, and seating myself upon a rock I laid before God my deep necessities, and besought His help. After a short time, seeing a poor man coming towards me I thought he had come to ask me for some relief because he was hungry and cold. I said to him, "I am a poor man, and except for this blanket I have nothing at all. You had better go to the village near by and ask for help there." And lo! even whilst I was saying this he flashed forth like lightning, and, showering drops of blessing, immediately disappeared. Alas! Alas! it was now clear to me that this was my beloved Master who came not to beg from a poor creature like me, but to bless and to enrich me (II Corinthians 8:9), and so I was left weeping and lamenting my folly and lack of insight.

On another day, my work being finished, I again

went into the forest to pray, and seated upon that same rock began to consider for what blessings I should make petition. Whilst thus engaged, it seemed to me that another came and stood near me, who, judged by his bearing and dress and manner of speech, appeared to be a revered and devoted servant of God; but his eyes glittered with craft and cunning, and as he spoke he seemed to breathe an odour of hell.

He thus addressed me: "Holy and Honoured Sir, pardon me for interrupting your prayers and breaking in on your privacy; but it is one's duty to seek to promote advantage of others, and therefore I have come to lay an important matter before you. Your pure and unselfish life has made a deep impression not only upon me, but upon a great number of devout persons. But although, in the Name of God, you have sacrificed yourself, body and soul for others, you have never been truly appreciated. My meaning is that, being a Christian, only a few thousand Christians have come under your influence, and some even of these distrust you. How much better would it be if you became a Hindu or a Muslim and thus become a great leader indeed? They are in search of such a spiritual head. If you accept this suggestion of mine, then three hundred and ten millions of Hindus and Muslims will become your followers, and render you reverent homage."

As soon as I heard this, there rushed from my lips these words, "Thou Satan! get thee hence. I knew at once that thou wast a wolf in sheep's clothing! Thy one wish is that I should give up the cross and the narrow path that leads to life, and choose the broad road of death. My Master Himself is my lot and my portion, who Himself gave His life for me, and it behooves me to offer as a sacrifice my life and all I have to Him who is all in all to me. Get thee gone therefore, for with thee I have nothing to do."

Hearing this, he went off grumbling and growling in his rage....

(This is an excerpt from *At the Master's Feet* by Sadhu Sundar Singh, which is available from End-Time Handmaidens. See the advertisement in the back of this book.)

Satan seldom appears in an ugly and repulsive form. He wouldn't get many followers that way.

Hell Was Made for the Fallen Angels

The fallen angels have not only lost their own habitation (*oikia* which means "residence, family, home"), they have been cast down to hell (II Peter 2:4) where they are kept in chains of darkness, detained until the judgment (*krisis* which means "condemnation, accusation, damnation, judgment").

The creation of hell was not in God's original plan. It was the solution to a problem, an afterthought. It was prepared for the devil and his angels (Matthew 25:41). It is a place of everlasting fire. The unrighteous people who follow Satan will end up there just like the angels did. For if God spared not the angels that sinned, but cast them down to hell, the false prophets, false teachers and those who follow them will surely be damned (II Peter 2:1-3).

Satan cannot deceive any more angels. He no longer has that power nor ability. The two thirds of the heavenly hosts that never sided with him when Satan instigated insurrection in Heaven have stayed loyal to God and fought His battles against Satan ever since. Today Satan uses persons to instigate insurrection in homes, churches, Christian organizations and even nations. He is still successful in gaining followers among the proud, the rebellious, the angry and the malcontents. They are influenced by their own evil hearts and Satan's deceptive lies to them. Darkness enters into their hearts and minds. When that darkness is full, it is impossible to lead them again to repentance. So they ultimately die, believing a lie. Only on the judgment day will they be able to acknowledge the truth. Then it will be too late (Hebrews 6:4-6).

Even as Lucifer was created by God (Ezekiel 28:13, 15), so all the heavenly hosts were created by Him.

Bible scholars disagree on whether or not the fallen angels and the demon or evil spirits are the same. The angels have bodies which God created for them. The demon spirits are disembodied spirits. If they are the same, how can they be active when God has reserved them in chains of darkness? On the other hand, if the demon spirits are creatures other than fallen angels, where did these demon spirits come from? Some say they are the spirits of a pre-adamic race. The Bible does not say where the demons originated, but it does say that the fallen angels fight the good angels under their captain the "dragon" (Revelation 12:7), and in Matthew 25:41, Jesus calls them the "devil's angels" implying that they still are under his control.

STUDY QUESTIONS

1. Why was one third of the angels cast out of Heaven?

2. What was Lucifer's position in Heaven?

3. Read Isaiah 14 and Ezekiel 28.

4. What does the word "transformed" in II Corinthians 11:14 mean?

5. Why did God create hell?

6. Many Bible scholars believe that there is a difference between demons and fallen angels. What is this difference?

7. Memorize Jude 6.

CHAPTER THREE

RANKS OF ANGELS

There is no doubt that there are different ranks and offices of angels. Just like there are different degrees of honour and position in human life, such as kings, presidents, ambassadors, servants, etc., the higher ranking angels are called archangels.

Michael

Jude 9 tells us that Michael is an Archangel. The word "archangel" comes from the Greek word *archaggelos*, consisting of two words *arche* which means "first in time or rank, and *aggelos*, "angel or messenger." An archangel is an angel who is at the top of the angelic ranks. He has this high position because of his virtue, his special services to God and probably because of his past record of loyalty and trustworthiness.

Michael has been given the title, "Prince of Israel" (Daniel 10:13, 21). In Revelation 12:7 and Daniel 12:1, he is named the great warring prince who will lead the armies of Heaven in the last days. *"And at that time shall Michael stand up, the great prince which standeth for the children of thy people: and there shall be a time of trouble, such as never was since there was a nation even to that same time: and at that time thy people shall be delivered, everyone that shall be found written in the book."* (Daniel 12:1) He is the one that fights the battles of Israel today. When terrorists hijack Israel's planes or planes with Israelis on board, they have to deal with Michael, the Prince of Israel. That is why it appears as though the Israeli intelligence is so excellent and why her army is invincible. While it is true they work hard at learning warfare, the real secret of their success is more than human; much can be accredited to the help they have from the unseen hosts who fight for them under their commander, Prince Michael, who has never lost a battle.

Because we Gentiles, through Christ, have been grafted into the "olive tree" of Israel and become "partakers of the root and fatness (ie. the inheritance and blessings) of the "olive tree" (Israel), we can claim the promises of Israel like any adopted child. *"And if some of the branches be broken off, and thou, being a wild olive tree, wert graffed in among them, and with them partakest of the root and fatness of the olive tree;"* (Romans 11:17). On this authority, we can rightfully trust that Prince Michael will honour our position in God's plan of salvation and fight for us just like he fights for Israel.

In these last days as the fullness of the Gentiles comes to a close (Romans 11:25), and the Lord is grafting Israel back into their own natural olive tree (Romans 11:24), we will be included, not only in the "root and fatness" (inheritance and blessings) of Israel, but we will also be identified with the warfare that Satan has waged against Israel through the years. It is interesting to observe how people want the glory that rests on Israel, but are unwilling to share in her trials, her testings and her rejection. This is so much a fact that some of God's people even reject natural Israel completely and only accept "spiritual" Israel. They even go so far as to teach and believe that the Jewish people are not of the stock of Israel. This error has entered the Christian church in a greater degree than imaginable. While I was in Australia, I had the privilege of receiving, in two tapes, a teaching against this so-called

"British Israel" teaching called *Bursting the Bubble of British Israelism* by the late Dr. Duff Forbes. I would be glad to share these tapes with anyone who is interested. (See the advertisement in the back of this book.) This man has made a complete study on this error and clearly points out the errors of this teaching. Because this Bible study is not on this subject, I do not want to go into it in any more detail here. Suffice it to say, we can claim the blessed help of Michael the Prince of Israel, who *"stands for the children of thy people"* (ie. Israel). We know he will rise up in the time of Jacob's trouble and deliver them (Daniel 12:1). But woe unto us if we find ourselves fighting against God's plan to graft Israel back into God's eternal plan of salvation. I fear for those who hate Israel and fight against her. They are fighting, not only little Judah, but the mighty warring Prince Michael, and all his warring angels who are under his command.

Gabriel

While both Jewish and Christian tradition name four Archangels, Michael, Gabriel, Raphael and Uriel, the Protestant Bible only names two: Michael the warring Prince, and Gabriel the Messenger Prince, God's Ambassador of Peace. Michael means "who is like God?" Gabriel means "God is powerful."

It is interesting to see how both of these names bring honour only to God and not to the angelic princes who bear them. That is the secret of true greatness.

Gabriel was called upon to explain to Daniel the vision concerning the nations (Daniel 8:16). Again in Daniel 9:20 Gabriel came while Daniel was praying, repenting and confessing his sins and the sins of his people Israel, and

19

presenting his supplication before the Lord his God. Daniel writes, *"Yea, while I was speaking in prayer, even the man Gabriel, whom I had seen in the vision at the beginning, being caused to fly swiftly, touched me about the time of the evening oblation. And he informed me, and talked with me, and said, O Daniel, I am now come forth to give thee skill and understanding."* (Daniel 9:21-22) Then, Gabriel proceeds to teach Daniel prophecy.

By this we see that Gabriel is the prince of skill, understanding and revelatory knowledge. In Daniel 9:25 he gives the exact time when Israel should expect their Messiah which was also fulfilled accordingly.

It is therefore right that when the time for the Messiah's birth came that Gabriel should have been the one to make this great announcement to both Zacharias (Luke 1:19) and Mary (Luke 1:26).

"And the angel answering said unto him, I am Gabriel, that stand in the presence of God; and am sent to speak unto thee, and to show thee these glad tidings." (Luke 1:19)

"And in the sixth month the angel Gabriel was sent from God unto a city of Galilee, named Nazareth, To a virgin espoused to a man whose name was Joseph, of the house of David; and the virgin's name was Mary." (Luke 1:26, 27)

Gabriel is undoubtedly the one who will blow the trumpet that is mentioned in I Thessalonians 4:16 and give the timely shout that will be God's sounding alarm for the resurrection of the dead and the rapture of the saints. I believe that Gabriel will be very much in charge of carrying out God's orders for the timely events of the future as listed in the prophetic Book of Revelation. He is going to be a busy angel!

It is encouraging to know he is the angel who supervises God's prophets and who touches them and imparts to them skill and understanding concerning the secrets which God wants to impart to men.

In the same way that people have different skills, gifts and callings, God's angels also have different gifts, skills and callings. It is quite possible that as Michael is active when God's saints are engaged in warfare, even so Gabriel is active and present when important revelatory and prophetic words are being spoken or written. One might say they are the patrons of war and wisdom.

Raphael

In addition let me just share a little about Raphael and Uriel. Raphael means "God has healed, God is the healer." He could be the angel who troubled (stirred) the waters of the Pool of Bethesda, thus bringing healing to the sick and lame who waited there, hoping for a miracle cure (John 5:1-4). If this is true, then Raphael will have a great part to play in the healing of the nations in the end-time.

We first read about Raphael in the Book of Tobit, chapters nine and ten. This is one of the Apocryphal books in the Protestant Bible, but it is accepted as canonical by the Roman Catholics. (See the advertisement in the back of this book.)

Tobit was one of the children of Israel from the tribe of Naphtali who was carried to Nineveh during the early captivity. In this story, he must send his son Tobias on a long journey. Raphael, acting as a human, accompanies him, guiding and protecting him. He also arranges a marriage for him with Sarah, a near kinswoman whom he delivers of an evil spirit. On their return, he heals Tobias' father, Tobit, who is blind. When they try to pay him a wage for his travel, he refuses it and tells them that he is Raphael and that he stands in the presence of God.

Uriel

Uriel, the last of the four great archangels, means "God is my light and my fire, light or fire of God, the one who has been illuminated by God." He is also named in the Apocrypha Book of II Esdras.

When the prophet Ezra and his companions challenged the angel Uriel with hard questions he answered them this: *"Come then, weigh me a pound of fire, measure me a bushel of wind, or call back a day that has passed."* (II Esdras 4:5) Uriel revealed many mysteries, secrets and hard riddles to Ezra. For the complete story read II Esdras 3-9.

In the teachings of the Catholic Church, he is believed to be the angel who stood at the gate of the Garden of Eden with the flaming sword. *Hastings' Bible Dictionary* identifies him as one of the angels who helped to bury Adam and Abel, the angel who wrestled with Jacob at Peniel, the destroyer of the Army of Sennacherib (II Kings 19:35), who killed 185,000, the messenger who warned Noah of the coming deluge (Enoch I, 10:1-3). He is supposed to have led Abraham out of Ur of the Chaldees. The Roman Catholic Church has given him sainthood and his symbol is an open hand holding a flame.

Uriel could be the angel referred to in Revelation 14:18, *"And another angel came out from the altar, which had power over fire;..."* The word "power" is *exousia* in Greek. It means "permission, authority, right, liberty." This great angel of Revelation 14-18 has the authority to pour out the fire of God upon the wicked end-time generation which blatantly flaunts their sins of sodomy, child abuse (the most abused are male children, 1 to 3 years of age), murder of infants (also called abortion), satanism, whoredom, adultery and pornography, besides many others. The wrath of God will fall like fire from

Heaven upon our sinful cities, towns and villages just like it did in the days of Sodom and Gomorrah. This angel, Uriel, could, I believe, be the angel who shall be the one in charge of carrying out God's orders. Woe unto the inhabitants of the earth when these four mighty angels work together in unity to judge the earth with the inhabitants thereof. But there is comfort in knowing that the judgment of God will be "without the city." *The winepress was trodden without the city, and blood came out of the winepress, even unto the horse bridles, by the space of a thousand and six hundred furlongs."* (Revelation 14:20) God's city, His people, the Holy City, the New Jerusalem which John saw coming down out of Heaven (Revelation 21:2) as a Bride prepared for her Bridegroom will be spared this terrible judgment. God and His mighty angels know who God«s people are. They will not be our enemy on that day if we live under the covenant of holiness and righteousness, trusting in His Blood. But if we live like the wicked, we will be destroyed together with them.

The Watchers

Even now the angels with the "slaughter weapons" in their hands are drawing nigh. God will soon command them to *"smite: let not your eye spare, neither have ye pity: Slay utterly old and young, both maids, and little children, and women: but come not near any man upon whom is the mark; and begin at my sanctuary."* (Ezekiel 9:2−6) But thanks be to God, in the midst of this scene of blood and anger and horror I see one "clothed in linen, with an inkhorn by his side and the Lord has said to him, *"...Go through the midst of the city, through the midst of Jerusalem, and set a mark upon the foreheads of the men that sigh and that cry for all the abominations that be done in the midst thereof."* (Verse 4) And to them who are given the command to wipe out a generation is also given the command, *"...but come not near any man upon whom is the mark;..."* (verse 6).

The thing that will mark us out for angelic preservation in the time of judgment is our life of holiness and intercession. The call of the Spirit has gone out for intercessors. *"Sigh therefore, thou son of man, with the breaking of thy loins; and with bitterness sigh before their eyes....A sword, a sword is sharpened, and also furbished: It is sharpened to make a sore slaughter;...And he hath given it to be furbished, that it may be handled: this sword is sharpened, and it is furbished, to give it into the hand of the slayer."* (Ezekiel 21:6—11)

I believe that the angelic hosts are marking out and writing down the names of the righteous. They are walking among the sons of men and recording the names of the righteous. They are the "watchers" that visited Sodom and determined its destruction, and also the "watchers" of Daniel 4:13, 17 who warned Nebuchadnezzar of his proud, boastful attitude and who later, in judgment, "hewed down his tree," causing him to become a madman for seven years until he was humbled and turned his eyes to Heaven at which time his understanding was restored to him and he gave glory to God and was restored to the throne of Babylon.

I believe these watchers are watching the thrones and governments of the world. They are passing judgment. Many are falling. Proud men are either falling from power overnight or being assassinated. The watchers are watching. They are the holy angels who are involved in the politics of the nations.

The Nations Have Guardian Angels

Even as there are principalities and powers, rulers of the darkness of this world and spiritual wickedness in high places (Ephesians 6:12), so there are the same different ranks in the angelic hosts. Every country has a mighty guardian angel over it. The first president of USA, George Washington, tells how he was visited by the "Angel of the Union" who gave him a prophetic vision of the United States — all of which has been fulfilled up to the present time; and no doubt that which remains to be fulfilled will also take place. (See the following chapter).

In this same way that the nations have guardian angels over them, Satan, who copies everything God does, also has ruling princes of darkness whom he has set over the nations to destroy them. In Daniel 10:13 we read how one of these ruling princes, the prince of Persia, sought to keep the Jews from being restored to their homeland after the 70 years of captivity; and Michael, the holy prince of Israel, fought the demonic prince of Persia until the victory was won. It was Daniel's fasting and interceding that brought the victory for Israel. Michael not only fought the demonic Prince of Persia, he also stayed with the Kings of Persia until Cyrus decreed the release and the return of the Jews to their land. The angels stay on the job until they have won the victory.

Seven Great Angels

In Revelation we read about there being seven great angels who will be very active in the last days as God pours His wrath out on the world. Raphael identified himself as, *"I am Raphael, one of the seven angels who stand in attendance on the Lord and enter his glorious presence."* (Tobit 12:15)

If then there are seven great angels (as some believe), rather than only four, who are they? We have already listed:

1. Michael, the warring angel
2. Gabriel, the messenger of skill, wisdom and divine revelation
3. Raphael, the healing and guiding angel
4. Uriel, the angel in command of light and fire.

That leaves three more. Scholars disagree on who they are, but the names of Raguel, Saraquel, Ramiel (or Camael), Anael (Haniel), Zadkiel, Orifiel and Uzzuel (or Sidriel) and others are listed by church historians as being names of powerful angels. I really don't think it is very important for us to know all this. It is interesting, but inspired Scripture does not mention all these names, even though there are many unnamed angels in the Bible.

STUDY QUESTIONS

1. What is an archangel?
2. What are the three characteristics that determine the angels' rank?
3. What is the Archangel Michael's task?
4. Why can we claim Michael's help?
5. Why was the Archangel Gabriel the one to announce the births of John the Baptist and Jesus?
6. What are the names of the other two archangels recorded in historic writings?
7. Read the Book of Daniel.
8. Memorize Daniel 12:1.

CHAPTER FOUR

WASHINGTON'S VISION

Because of the strategic hour that we are living in and the importance of the vision which God gave President George Washington, I feel it should be included in this Bible study. It also validates the fact that all nations have guardian angels just like Israel has Michael.

In the book *George Washington, the Christian* we find some interesting details about the life of America's greatest man and prophet of God. It tells about a council that took place at the junction of the Kanawah and Ohio Rivers in 1770 (15 years after the Battle of the Monongahela River during the French and Indian War of 1755). The parties at this council were George Washington, his friend Dr. Craik and the Indians who were headed by their chief. The chief told them, that during the battle he had commanded a firing squad of young Indian sharpshooters to bring Washington down as he rode the lines, attempting to rally British and Colonial troops. However, it was suddenly impossible for them to hit their mark. The chief concluded by saying this: "T'was all in vain; a power mightier far than we shielded him from harm. He cannot die in battle. I am old, and soon shall be gathered to the great council fire of my fathers in the land of shades, but ere I go, there is something that bids me speak in the voice of prophecy: Listen! The Great Spirit protects that man, and guides his destinies — he will become the chief of nations, and a people yet unborn will hail him as the founder of a mighty empire."

George Washington was born on February 22, 1732. Few military figures in history ever faced misery and deprivation as did Washington and his forces at Valley Forge in the winter of 1777-1778. But three years later British General Charles Cornwallis surrendered to Washington at Yorktown to end the American Revolutionary War.

The following is a well-documented accounting of a vision General Washington had at Valley Forge.

Anthony Sherman

More than a century ago a Mr. Wesley Bradshaw published an article in which he quoted Anthony Sherman, who was an officer with General George Washington at Valley Forge.

Bradshaw's original article was reprinted in the *National Tribune*, Vol. 4, No. 12, for December, 1880. He told of the last time he saw Anthony Sherman, and these are Bradshaw's words:

The last time I ever saw Anthony Sherman was on the fourth of July, 1859, in Independence Square. He was then ninety-nine years old, and becoming very feeble. But though so old, his dimming eyes rekindled as he gazed upon Independence Hall, which he came to visit once more.

"Let us go into the hall," he said. "I want to tell you of an incident of Washington's life — one which no one alive knows of except myself; and, if you will, before long, see it verified.

"From the opening of the Revolution we experienced all phases of fortune, now good and now ill, one time victorious and another conquered. The darkest period we had, I think, was when Washington after several reverses retreated to Valley Forge, where he resolved to pass the winter of 1777. Ah! I have often seen the tears coursing down our dear commander's care-worn cheeks, as he would be conversing with a confidential officer about the condition of his poor soldiers. You have doubtless heard the story of Washington's going into the thicket to pray. Well, it was not only true, but he used often to pray in secret for aid and comfort from God, the interposition of whose Divine Providence brought us safely through the darkest days of tribulation.

"One day, I remember it well, the chilly winds whistled through the leafless trees, though the sky was cloudless and the sun shone brightly, he remained in his quarters nearly all the afternoon alone. When he came out I noticed that his face was a shade paler than usual, and there seemed to be something on his mind of more than ordinary importance. Returning just after dusk, he dispatched an orderly to the quarters of the officer I mentioned who was presently in attendance. After a preliminary conversation of about half an hour, Washington, gazing upon his companion with that strange look of dignity which only he alone could command, said to the latter:

" 'I do not know whether it is owing to an anxiety of my mind, or what, but this afternoon as I was sitting at this table engaged in preparing a dispatch, something seemed to disturb me. Looking up, I beheld standing opposite me a singularly beautiful female. So astonished was I, for I had given strict orders not to be disturbed, that it was some moments before I found language to

29

inquire into the cause of her presence. A second, a third, and even a fourth time did I repeat my question, but received no answer from my mysterious visitor except a slight raising of her eyes. By this time I felt strange sensations spreading through me. I would have risen but the riveted gaze of the being before me rendered volition impossible. I assayed once more to address her, but my tongue had become useless. Even thought itself had become paralyzed. A new influence, mysterious, potent, irresistible, took possession of me. All I could do was to gaze steadily, vacantly at my unknown visitor. Gradually, the surrounding atmosphere seemed as though becoming filled with sensations, and luminous. Everything about me seemed to rarify; the mysterious visitor herself becoming more airy and yet more distinct to my sight than ever before. I now began to feel as one dying, or rather to experience the sensations which I have sometimes imagined accompany dissolution. I did not think, I did not reason, I did not move; all were alike impossible. I was only conscious of gazing fixedly, vacantly at my companion.

The First Peril

" 'Presently I heard a voice saying, "Son of the Republic, look and learn," while at the same time my visitor extended her arm eastwardly. I now beheld a heavy white vapor at some distance rising fold upon fold. This gradually dissipated, and I looked upon a strange scene. Before me lay, spread out in one vast plain, all the countries of the world — Europe, Asia, Africa and America. I saw rolling and tossing between

30

Europe and America the billows of the Atlantic, and between Asia and America lay the Pacific. "Son of the Republic," said the same mysterious voice as before, "Look and learn." At that moment I beheld a dark, shadowy being, like an angel, standing, or rather floating in mid-air, between Europe and America. Dipping water out of the ocean in the hollow of each hand, he sprinkled some upon America with his right hand, while with his left hand he cast some on Europe. Immediately a cloud raised from these countries, and joined in mid-ocean. For a while it remained stationary, and then moved slowly westward, until it enveloped America in its murky folds. Sharp flashes of lightning gleamed through it at intervals, and I heard the smothered groans and cries of the American people.

" 'A second time the angel dipped water from the ocean, and sprinkled it out as before. The dark cloud was then drawn back to the ocean, in whose heaving billows it sank from view.

The Growth of America

" 'A third time I heard the mysterious voice saying, "Son of the Republic, look and learn." I cast my eyes upon America and beheld villages and towns and cities springing up one after another until the whole land from the Atlantic to the Pacific was dotted with them. Again, I heard the mysterious voice say, "Son of the Republic, the end of the century cometh, look and learn."

31

The Second Peril

" 'At this the dark shadowy angel turned his face southward, and from Africa I saw an ill-omened spectre approach our land. It flitted slowly over every town and city of the latter. The inhabitants presently set themselves in battle array against each other. As I continued looking I saw a bright angel, on whose brow rested a crown of light, on which was traced the word "Union," bearing the American flag which he placed between the divided nation, and said, "Remember ye are brethren." Instantly, the inhabitants, casting away their weapons, became friends once more, and united around the National Standard.

The Third Peril

" 'And again I heard the mysterious voice saying, "Son of the Republic, look and learn." At this the dark, shadowy angel placed a trumpet to his mouth, and blew three distinct blasts; he sprinkled it upon Europe, Asia, and Africa. Then my eyes beheld a fearful scene: from each of these countries arose thick, black clouds that were soon joined into one. And throughout this mass there gleamed a dark red light by which I saw hordes of armed men, who, moving by with the cloud, marched by land and sailed by sea to America, which country was enveloped in the volume of cloud. And I dimly saw these vast armies devastate the whole country and burn villages, towns and cities that I beheld springing up. As my ears listened to the thundering of the cannon, clashing of swords, and the shouts and cries of millions in mortal combat, I heard again the mysterious voice saying, "Son of the Republic, look and learn." When the voice had ceased, the dark shadowy angel placed his trumpet once more to his mouth, and blew a long and fearful blast.

" 'Instantly a light as of a thousand suns shone from above me, and pierced and broke into fragments the dark cloud which enveloped America. At the same moment the angel upon whose head still shone the word "Union," and who bore our national flag in one hand and a sword in the other, descended from the heavens attended by legions of white spirits. These immediately joined the inhabitants of America, who I perceived were well-nigh overcome, but who immediately taking courage again, closed up their broken ranks and renewed the battle. Again, amid the fearful noise of the conflict, I heard the mysterious voice saying, "Son of the Republic, look and learn." As the voice ceased, the shadowy angel for the last time dipped water from the ocean and sprinkled it upon America. Instantly the dark cloud rolled back, together with the armies it had brought, leaving the inhabitants of the land victorious.

Final Peace

" 'Then once more I beheld the villages, towns and cities springing up where I had seen them before, while the bright angel, planting the azure standard he had brought in the midst of them, cried with a loud voice: "While the stars remain, and the heavens send down dew upon the earth, so long shall the Union last." And taking from his brow the crown on which blazoned the

33

word "Union," he placed it upon the Standard while the people, kneeling down, said, "Amen."

" 'The scene instantly began to fade and dissolve, and I at last saw nothing but the rising, curling vapor I at first beheld. This also disappearing I found myself once more gazing upon the mysterious visitor, who, in the same voice I had heard before, said, "Son of the Republic, what you have seen is thus interpreted: Three great perils will come upon the Republic. The most fearful is the third passing which the whole world united shall not prevail against her. Let every child of the Republic learn to live for his God, his land and Union." With these words the vision vanished, and I started from my seat and felt I had seen a vision wherein had been shown to me the birth, progress, and destiny of the United States.' "

A Word of Warning

Anthony Sherman climaxed his recollection of Washington's words by saying, "Such, my friends, were the words I heard from Washington's own lips, and America will do well to profit by them."

Thomas Jefferson once said of our first President: "His integrity was the most pure, his justice the most flexible, I have ever known. He was, indeed, in every sense of the word, a wise, a good and a great man."

Interpretation of the Vision

These three perils which George Washington saw all took place on American soil.

Peril 1: Was no doubt the revolutionary war which still continued for three years after the Lord gave Washington the vision. There was much suffering, but not as intense as the other perils which were yet to come.

Peril 2: The ill-omened spectre coming from Africa points towards slavery as the issue of a terrible civil conflict when the nation was divided and brothers fought brothers.

Peril 3: The last and most terrible of all, clearly predicts hordes of enemies from Europe, Asia and Africa, armed for mortal combat. A red light accompanies these terrible invaders – indicating they are no doubt Communists. They come by air (the cloud), land (perhaps via Canada or Mexico and Central America) and sea. They devastate all of America, destroying cities, towns and villages. Millions are engaged in mortal conflict. Just when all seems lost, divine intervention from Heaven, angels and saints descend to assist the inhabitants of America to close their ranks and win the final victory.

A special warning is given by the Angel of the Union to Americans: "LET EVERY CHILD OF THE REPUBLIC LEARN TO LIVE FOR HIS GOD, HIS LAND, AND UNION." This is an indication that in the last peril patriotism, the love of country, the respect for our constitution and our faith in God will be in great jeopardy. Already we find this to be the case. May God help us to heed the warning of the Guardian Angel of America – before it's too late!

The two World Wars and the Korean and Vietnam wars were never shown to Washington. Probably because they were not fought on American soil.

35

STUDY QUESTIONS

1. Describe the three perils in George Washington's vision.

2. What is the interpretation of the vision?

CHAPTER FIVE

THE PURPOSE OF THE CREATION OF ANGELS AND THEIR DIFFERENT MINISTRIES

Although angels are very active in warfare this was not the original reason for their creation. God created them for the purpose of companionship, as an act of love and life, for life must always procreate. They were created to worship the Lord and to be a joy to Him forever. The angels are "lovers." They were never made to fight. But, because of the fall, they have had to engage in warfare, first to defend the Throne of God and then to protect God's creation, the earth and man, who is made in the image of God.

I. Angels Were Created to Worship.

The angels excel in worship and praise. From the smallest to the greatest, their whole life is one of praise to God. David, the praiser, discovered this secret and shared it with us in the Psalms.

Psalm 103:20, *"Bless the Lord, ye his angels, that excel in strength, that do his commandments, hearkening unto the voice of his word."*

And again in Psalm 148:2, *"Praise ye him, all his angels; praise ye him, all his hosts."*

John, the revelator also saw the angels worshipping in Heaven. Revelation 5:11-12, 7:11-12, *"And I beheld, and I heard the voice of many angels round about the throne, and the beasts, and the elders: and the number of them was ten*

*thousand times ten thousand, and thousands of thousands;
Saying with a loud voice, Worthy is the Lamb that was slain
to receive power, and riches, and wisdom, and strength, and
honour, and glory, and blessing.... And all the angels stood
round about the throne, and about the elders and the four
beasts, and fell before the throne on their faces, and
worshipped God, Saying, Amen: Blessing, and glory, and
wisdom, and thanksgiving, and honour, and power, and might,
be unto our God for ever and ever. Amen."*

This is how the angels worship the Lord God. Perhaps
we would do well to learn from them. The angels have much
to teach us humans in love, humility and purity.

II. Angels Are the Guardians — Cherubim

Angels are the guardians of Heaven. The first word we
have of angels is in Genesis 3:24 where God sent Adam and
Eve out of the Garden of Eden; in order to prevent their re-
entry, He placed at the east of the Garden of Eden cherubim
(plural for cherub), and a flaming sword which turned every
way to keep the way of the tree of life.

Some Bible scholars believe that the cherubim are an
order of angels which rank below the seraphim.

Cherubim, carved of wood and covered with gold, were
placed over the Ark of the Covenant, both in the tabernacle
in the wilderness (Exodus 25:22, Numbers 7:89), and in
Solomon's temple (I Kings 6:29, 32; 7:36). The cherubim
in Solomon's temple must have been very magnificent. Their
wingspan stretched about 15 feet from the tip of one cherub
wing to the far tip of the other. Only the high priest was
permitted to enter the Holy of Holies. So generations of
Israelites never saw this beautiful sight. The cherubim,
described by Ezekiel and in Ezekiel's temple (Ezekiel 41:18-20,

25) which has never yet been constructed, resemble more the four living creatures of Revelation (compare Revelation 4:6-8 and Ezekiel 1:5-12). Both had the same four faces of a man, an ox (calf), a lion and an eagle. This is symbolic of the four Gospels which record the life of Jesus from four different aspects.

Matthew portrays Jesus as the **Lion** of the tribe of Judah, the King of Israel.

Mark portrays Him as the **Servant**. The ox or the calf was the serving beast of the household of the farmer in Israel.

Luke portrays Jesus as the **Man**. His humanity is so beautifully revealed through Luke.

John portrays Jesus as the **Eagle** who soars to the highest Heaven as we see Him as the Son of God.

The cherubim and seraphim have the same attributes as our Lord. These are attributes which should be in the life of every child of God. If we are to be like Jesus, we should be able to rule with Him (the Lion), serve with Him (the Ox), walk the dusty roads of life with Him (the Man) and rise into the heavens and be seated in heavenly places with Him (the Eagle).

While all angels are the guardians of Heaven, the cherubim seem to have this duty and calling more than any other rank.

1. They guard the tree of life. We see the cherubim with the sword of fire are the guardians of the tree of life. They are responsible for preventing man from gaining access to secrets, thus keeping him from living forever in his sins. It could possibly be therefore that they have the authority to cut the "silver cord of life" and are responsible for ushering souls into the presence of God.

2. They guarded the ark of the covenant and the mercy

seat (Exodus 25:18-22, 37:7-9). When Moses was instructed to place the cherubim over the Mercy Seat, it was only a type of the real true office work of this angelic rank. They were guardians of the shekinah of glory, not only in the Holy of Holies, but also in the Heavenlies. The precious treasure of the Holy of Holies was the glory of God. That is the key to life, even eternal life. The death sentence came upon man because he lost the glory of God when he sinned. *"For all have sinned, and come short of (failed) the glory of God."* (Romans 3:23) Here again, we see the cherubim guarding the glory of God, which is the "cure" for death.

3. The cherubim guard the Throne of God in Heaven where His immediate presence is and the seat of His power. The earthly is only a type of the heavenly. Psalm 80:1 says, *Give ear, O Shepherd of Israel, thou that leadest Joseph like a flock; thou that dwellest between the cherubim, shine forth."*

Psalm 99:1, *"The Lord reigneth; let the people tremble: he sitteth between the cherubims; let the earth be moved."*

There are four living creatures which John saw, *"And before the throne there was a sea of glass like unto crystal. And in the midst of the throne, and round about the throne, were four beasts full of eyes before and behind. And the first beast was like a lion, and the second beast like a calf, and the third beast had a face as a man, and the fourth beast was like a flying eagle."* (Revelation 4:6-7) John saw these angels hovering over the Throne in actuality which the furnishings of the temple had depicted typologically. John saw them in their service as guardians of the Throne, *"And the four beasts had each of them six wings about him; and they were full of eyes within: and they rest not day and night, saying, Holy, holy, holy, Lord God Almighty, which was, and is, and is to come."* (Revelation 4:8) When these guardian

40

angels gave glory and honour and thanks to Him that sat on the throne, then all of Heaven was moved to worship Him and cast their crowns down before Him.

4. The cherubim are the guardians of Jerusalem and the government of Israel (Ezekiel 10:1-22). In Ezekiel 10 we read a remarkable account of the activity of the cherubim in regard to the city of Jerusalem and the government of Judah. Ezekiel sees more than a natural throne of Israel. He sees the actual Throne of God from whence Jerusalem was supposed to be governed, had she been faithful to God. He hears the cherubim that are resting above a throne that had the brilliance of a sapphire gemstone speak to a man clothed in linen and saying, *"...Go in between the wheels, even under the cherub, and fill thine hand with coals of fire from between the cherubim, and scatter them over the city..."* (Ezekiel 10:2)

"And one cherub stretched forth his hand from between the cherubim unto the fire that was between the cherubim, and took thereof, and put it into the hands of him that was clothed with linen; who took it, and went out." (Ezekiel 10:7) Immediately after that the glory of God departs from the temple and the city of Jerusalem is left without divine protection. Consequently, Nebuchadnezzar's army is free to totally destroy it, which is what happened.

So we see, the cherubim are the protectors of thrones, governments and ruling powers that operate under God. This includes great religious institutions like Judaism and Christianity. But when sin causes God's glory to depart, the cherubim themselves will put the coals of the fire of God's wrath in the hand of the man clothed with linen who shall pour out God's fire upon the guilty, causing their destruction. It is a terrible thing when a ruler's body guards arc the ones who put him to death. If, because of our sin, God cannot protect our nation any longer, then the same angels who are the guardians of our union will pour God's wrath upon us. Always remember the guardian has the right and the responsibility to correct the wayward and rebellious child.

5. The great tribulation — Revelation 8:1-5. The great tribulation with the terrible judgments will begin right after the angel takes the censer, fills it with the fire of the heavenly altar and casts it into the earth. This outpouring of God's wrath in the form of thunderings, lightnings and earthquakes resulting in terrible destruction, many believe, will also release the final great revival and harvest of souls. Certainly we know there will be two great end-time harvests that will take place simultaneously. One of souls coming into the Kingdom of God and one of souls who will be cast into hell (Joel 3:9-15, 18; Revelation 14:14-20).

III. Seraphim

The angelic rank of seraphim is mentioned by Isaiah in Isaiah 6:2, 6 about 640 BC. *"Above it stood the seraphims: each one had six wings; with twain he covered his face, and with twain he covered his feet, and with twain he did fly....Then flew one of the seraphims unto me, having a live coal in his hand, which he had taken with the tongs from off the altar:"*

Here we see that these same glorious creatures stood above the throne of God, even like the cherubim; and like the cherubim they had the power and authority to touch the live coals of fire from the altar and use it as God desired. This time, the fire from the altar did not destroy Isaiah; it only destroyed his sin and uncleanness, so that he could become a pure vessel to deliver a pure message. Many of

God's servants need to be cleansed with the coals from off the altar so that they can again be God's prophets to the nations. Too many are answering the call without a work of sanctification having been done in their lives. Therefore they produce unclean prophets in the land, even prophets after their own kind.

The word *seraphim* is plural for *saraph* in Hebrew which means "to be on fire, to burn, to absorb with fire." They glowed like fire with a brilliancy that was symbolic of the courts of Heaven.

STUDY QUESTIONS

1. For what purpose were angels created?

2.　Memorize Psalm 103:20.

3. What is the difference between the cherubim and seraphim?

4. In which different ways do the gospels portray Jesus?

5. In what way are angels involved in the great tribulation?

CHAPTER SIX

MINISTRIES OF ANGELS IN REGARD TO CHRIST

Up to now we have mostly studied the office work of the angels in regard to their ministry to God and His Throne. But angels also were assigned to minister to Christ. The writer of Hebrews had a very great understanding about the ministry of the angels. Read the first chapter. Now let us look at it more closely.

1. Hebrews 1:4-6: *"Being made so much better than the angels, as he hath by inheritance obtained a more excellent name than they. For unto which of the angels said he at any time, Thou art my Son, this day have I begotten thee? And again, I will be to him a Father, and he shall be to me a Son? And again, when he bringeth in the first-begotten into the world, he saith, And let all the angels of God worship him."* We understand from Psalm 8:5 that man was made a *"little lower than the angels."* In this verse (Hebrews 1:4) we understand that the Son of God was *"...made so much better than the angels, as he hath by inheritance obtained a more excellent name than they. For unto which of the angels said he at any time, Thou art my Son, this day have I begotten thee?"*

The angels were commissioned to attend the birth of the Christ child on that first Christmas eve long ago when the skies above Bethlehem rang with the praises of ten thousand times ten thousand and thousands of thousands of angels (Revelation 5) who left Heaven's corridors and came sweeping down through the starry space to sing the first Christmas herald, *"Glory to God in the highest, and on earth peace, good will toward men."* (Luke 2:14) They not only attended Jesus' birth; they ministered to Him throughout His earthly ministry.

2. The Angel of the Lord protected Jesus from Herod's jealous wrath by warning Joseph to take the young child and His mother and flee into Egypt. (Matthew 2:13)

3. When Herod died, the angel again appeared to Joseph in a dream and gave him orders to return to the land of Israel, telling him, *"...they are dead which sought the young child's life."* (Matthew 2:20)

I am sure that as a child He heard His mother and Joseph talk about these experiences. It must have made a great impression on Him.

4. After Jesus had fasted forty days in the wilderness and Satan had unsuccessfully tempted Him, the angels came and ministered unto Him (Matthew 4:11).

5. When Jesus was praying on the Mount of Olives on the eve of His crucifixion, He entered into great agony of soul travail. In His darkest hour right after He prayed, *"...not my will, but thine, be done...there appeared an angel unto him from heaven, strengthening him."* (Luke 22:43)

6. Later, when the temple guard came to arrest Him, and Peter, in great agitation, raised his sword and cut off the ear of one of the high priest's servants, Jesus rebuked Peter, saying, *"...Put up again thy sword into his place: for all they that take the sword shall perish with the sword. Thinkest thou that I cannot now pray to my Father, and he shall presently give me more than twelve legions of angels?"* (Matthew 26:52, 53)

In Roman times a legion was the chief subdivision of the army, containing about 6,000 infantry, with a contingent of cavalry. Jesus knew that all Heaven stood in readiness, prepared to come at His slightest wish.

7. Angels attended the resurrection of Christ. It was an angel who rolled the stone back from the door of the tomb and sat upon it. *"...His countenance was like lightning, and his raiment white as snow: And for fear of him the keepers did shake, and became as dead men."* (Matthew 28:3-4) But to the humble women who had come early that morning to embalm His Body, the angel said, *"...Fear not ye: for I know that ye seek Jesus, which was crucified. He is not here: for he is risen, as he said. Come, see the place where the Lord lay. And go quickly, and tell his disciples that he is risen from the dead; and, behold, he goeth before you into Galilee; there shall ye see him: lo, I have told you."* (Verses 6 and 7)

Because it was a mighty angel and one who brought a very special announcement and he had *"descended from heaven"* (verse 2) to bring this message, I believe he must have been none other than the great Messenger Angel Gabriel who was very involved in the life of Jesus from the beginning.

8. That same morning Mary Magdalene *"...stood without at the sepulchre weeping: and as she wept, she stooped down, and looked into the sepulchre, And seeth two angels in white sitting, the one at the head, and the other at the feet, where the body of Jesus had lain. And they say unto her, Woman, why weepest thou?..."* (John 20:11-13) When she told them why, they did not explain to her about His resurrection like they did to the other women because they knew Jesus was still in the garden and He, Himself, would comfort her. Angels only do and say that which they have been commissioned of the Father.

9. Last of all, on the day of Christ's ascension, after giving the great commission, *"...Go ye into all the*

world, and preach the gospel to every creature'' (Mark 16:15), and commanding them to tarry in Jerusalem until they be endued with power from on high (Luke 24:49) because they would receive power after the Holy Ghost would come upon them which would enable them to be witnesses in Jerusalem and in all Judea and in Samaria, and unto the uttermost parts of the earth (Acts 1:8). He was taken up and a cloud received Him out of their sight. *''And while they looked steadfastly toward heaven as he went up, behold, two men stood by them in white apparel; Which also said, Ye men of Galilee, why stand ye gazing up into heaven? this same Jesus, which is taken up from you into heaven, shall so come in like manner as ye have seen him go into heaven.''* (Acts 1:10, 11)

These two men (*aner* in Greek) could have been either angels or glorified saints like Moses and Elijah who appeared to Him on the Mount of Transfiguration. They were certainly heavenly beings who did not have ordinary human bodies.

10. This concludes the angelic ministry in the earthly life of Jesus. But when He returns to earth, the angels will return with Him. Jesus Himself said, *''For the Son of man shall come in the glory of his Father with his angels;...''* (Matthew 6:27) And again in Matthew 25:31, 32 He said, *''When the Son of man shall come in his glory, and all the holy angels with him, then shall he sit upon the throne of his glory: And before him shall be gathered all nations:...''*

Mark 13:26, 27: *''And then shall they see the son of man coming in the clouds with great power and glory. And then shall he send his angels, and shall gather together his elect from the four winds, from the uttermost part of the earth to the uttermost part of heaven.''*

When He returns, not only will the angels accompany Him, but armies of saints, clothed in white linen, riding upon

48

white horses will follow Him out of the Heavens (Revelation 19:14, Jude 14).

Jesus' entire life was accompanied by angelic ministry. If this is true, we can expect that it should be normal for angels to minister to His followers also, for we are joint-heirs with Him of the promises of God. If Jesus needed their help and encouragement, how much more do we!

STUDY QUESTIONS

1. Memorize Hebrews 1:4-6.

2. Mention at least seven occasions in the life of Jesus when the angels ministered to Him.

3. Why did the angels not tell Mary Magdalene about the resurrection as they had to the other women?

4. Who will accompany Jesus at His return?

5. What shows how much we need angelic ministry?

CHAPTER SEVEN

ANGELS MINISTER TO HUMANS

Hebrews 1:14 clearly tells us that the angels have been commissioned by the Father to minister to us, *"Are they not all ministering spirits, sent forth to minister for them who shall be heirs of salvation?"*

The word "minister" is *oiakonia* in Greek which means "serviceable labour, assistance." It involved compassionate love. It is related to the word "deacon." The angels, therefore, are our heavenly "deacons" who are commissioned to serve us in great love and understanding.

Because the angels communicate with each other, one angel can tell another angel all about our needs. Our own personal "deacon" is our guardian angel who has been with us since our birth. They know everything there is to know about us − our virtues, our sins and weaknesses, our heredity, our environment, our God-given callings and talents, our likes and dislikes. Sometimes I think we become like our angels. Although I have never seen my own guardian angel, there are those who have. They have told me that my angel is a happy angel who loves adventure. (He needs to in order to live with me). Some have said there is a marked resemblance between my angel and me. I think that, if a person looks like the angel who is their guardian, then there could be times when people have thought they had seen a person, but instead they had only seen his angel.

Do We Resemble Our Guardian Angels?

When Peter was in prison and the early church was holding an all-night prayer meeting on his behalf, because he was sentenced to die the next day, the angel of the Lord released him and brought him out of prison. When he arrived at the house, the Christians thought it was his angel. So we see the people of that day accepted the fact that a person and his guardian angel resembled each other (Acts 12:15).

A pastor and his wife, whom I know and respect in the Lord, told me recently how they had had a dream that they cast an evil spirit out of a person. The amazing part of this account is that the evil spirit that came out of that person looked just like that one. Both of them had this same dream. This reminded me of an unpleasant experience I had some years ago when a violent spirit of anger and hatred came against me. This hate spirit was so strong that it tried to intimidate me. Every morning when I woke up, I would see that hate spirit leering at me from across the room. It was both frightening and sickening. My only refuge was in prayer and the covering of the Blood of Jesus and His mighty Name. The amazing thing was that this evil spirit of hate looked just like a man I had believed was a brother in Christ. He had been very "smooth" and "polite," saying nice words to me, but underneath his charming exterior was great hatred towards me. What puzzled me for years was the fact that the evil spirit from him resembled him exactly. It wasn't until I heard the testimony of my friends that I understood. We can become like the evil spirits that would seek to possess us or we can be pure and holy and take on the likeness of the beautiful heavenly angels, and even more, like our Lord Jesus Himself.

Angels Serve

Hebrews 1:7 tells us, *"And of the angels he saith, Who maketh his angels spirits, and his ministers a flame of fire."*

As we co-operate with the great angelic ministry in these last days, we, too, shall become his ministers who shall be as "a flame of fire." This is only as the fire of the Holy Ghost fills us and we become indeed baptized with the Holy Ghost and fire (Matthew 3:11) that we can be His ministers of fire. It pleases God to touch the lips of all of us whom He has called, with the coals of fire from the heavenly altar that we might be pure, clean and holy vessels which He can use in these last days.

It must grieve the ministering angels to see the unclean lives in the ministry and the impure vessels which God has to use because there are not enough Isaiahs in the land who are honest enough to cry out, *"Woe is me! for I am undone; because I am a man of unclean lips, and I dwell in the midst of a people of unclean lips:..."* (Isaiah 6:5)

Jesus, in His great humility, was willing to be made *"...a little lower than the angels;..."* when He *"took on him the seed of Abraham."* (Hebrews 2:9, 16) He did this only that he could *"taste death for every man."*

Yet, if angels still served and ministered to Jesus, even though for 33 years He was "lower" than them, because He confined Himself to a human, physical body, then we can expect that the angels will love us and minister to us even as they did to our "Brother" Jesus (Hebrews 2:11).

But, through the redeeming work of Jesus, we shall receive a new and wonderful resurrected body that will make us equal to the angels, for our bodies will be like those of the angels. Jesus explained this when He was asked a question about marriage relationships in Heaven, He said, *"The children of the world marry, and are given in marriage: But they which shall be accounted worthy to obtain that world, and the resurrection from the dead, neither marry, nor are given in marriage: Neither can they die any more: for they are **equal unto the angels*** (i.e. *isaggelos* in Greek: consisting of *isos*, "like" and *aggelos*, "angel"); *and are the children of God, being the children of the resurrection."* (Luke 20:34-36)

It is only as the glory of God is restored to us through par with angels in the physical sense. For then we will no more experience pain or great sorrow or death, but we will be immortal like the angels. We shall be co-heirs with Jesus Christ and one of our future responsibilities will be to judge the angels. *"Know ye not that we shall judge angels?..."* writes Paul in I Corinthians 6:3. It is not the good angels whom we shall judge. It is the fallen angels.

Angels are never permitted to pass judgment. That is reserved for Deity and for us also (as we have just read). II Peter 2:11 says, *"Whereas angels, which are greater in power and might, bring not railing accusation against them before the Lord."*

Jude 9 confirms this truth concerning Prince Michael in his dealings with the devil, *"Yet Michael the archangel, when contending with the devil he disputed about the body of Moses, durst not bring against him a railing accusation, but said, The Lord rebuke thee."*

However, the angels will witness the judgment and will be there in that dreadful day. (Matthew 25:31, Mark 8:38, Luke 9:26).

The angels will not be rulers in the "world to come." Hebrews 2:5: *"For unto the angels hath he not put in subjection the world to come,...''* No, instead it is man whom God has created to be ruler over this world and all His great created works. Hebrews 2:6-8, *"But one in a certain place testified, saying, What is man, that thou art mindful of him? or the son of man, that thou visitest him? Thou madest him a little lower than the angels; thou crownedst him with glory and honour, and didst set him over the works of thy hands; Thou hast put all things in subjection under his feet. For in that he put all in subjection under him, he left nothing that is not put under him. But now we see not yet all things put under him.''* Though we still do not see ourselves entering fully into this power and authority, we know it has been decreed and we shall rule and reign with Him. (Revelation 2:26; 3:21; 5:10; 20:6; 22:5).

During the millennia of the future, the great angelic hosts will be able to serve us in the way they were created to serve. Our sin and unbelief has hindered them from being all that they could be to us in the Kingdom. Instead of them using their time to help us rule, they are busy keeping us from sinning, protecting us from our foolish mistakes and working around our rebellious, stubborn ways. But when, and as, we become like Christ and wholly submitted to the will of God in everything we do, the angels will be able to team up with us like they did with great saints like Daniel, Moses, Ezekiel, Paul and John (who received the great revelation through the hand of an angel), and we will be the power for God which all the demons of hell and the wicked of this earth will never be able to get the victory over. The world has yet to meet up with triumphant host. May that day not be long hence!

55

STUDY QUESTIONS

1. Memorize Hebrews 1:13-14.

2. Which angel knows most about us?

3. What does it mean "to be equal unto the angels" (Luke 20:34-36)?

4. Are angels allowed to pass judgment? Why?

5. How can we become a team with the angels that will conquer the forces of hell?

CHAPTER EIGHT

QUESTIONS PEOPLE ASK ABOUT ANGELS

1. Do angels have wings?

This is one of the most frequently talked about subjects. The answer is yes and no. The cherubim and seraphim definitely do and many of the angels have wings. Others do not. They can choose to appear in the form of a person, dressed as a man or woman or even a child. Their clothing is usually inconspicuous, so as not to alert people as to who they are.

When my brother Jamie was very sick with a bad heart, diabetes, gout and high blood pressure, he lay in his hospital bed, suffering with thirst. All liquids had been refused him by the doctor. In his misery he cried out to God. Suddenly, a large angel flew through the walls of the hospital into his room. The angel called his name. Jamie saw he was holding a golden goblet in his hand. He told Jamie to drink as he poured from the goblet into my brother's mouth. Jamie said to me later, "I would recognize that angel anywhere. He had curly red hair, and a big smile. His wings were still stretched out and they were very large." When I asked him, "What do you think the angel gave you to drink?" he said, "New wine! I immediately fell asleep and when I woke up the next morning, I was well. The doctor could not find anything wrong with me." God added about five years to Jamie's life.

Barbara J., a young mother with several small children, was so overcome by the suffering and abuse — both physical and mental — which she and her children had received from her husband, their father, that she left with her children and drove from Canada to Florida to live with her parents.

But after some time there she suddenly left, without saying good-bye, to return to her husband. Her godly parents were greatly concerned as they felt she was making a bad mistake which would end in more suffering and tragedy.

On their trip back home, she and the children stopped to eat lunch. While the children were playing, she began to make sandwiches for them from the bread and supplies she had in the car.

Suddenly, a strange man appeared and asked her if she could give him some food. She kindly gave him the sandwich she had been making, telling him she was glad to do so.

He then ate it and said, "Are you Barbara?"

Surprised, she answered, "Yes."

Then he said, "You are planning on returning to your husband. Don't do it. You will only have grief and suffering and tragedy." Then he disappeared.

Barbara was shaken by what he had told her, but, hoping for the best, she continued driving north to her home in Canada.

The minute she arrived, she knew she had made a terrible mistake. She knew then that God had sent an angel to warn her.

She suffered much until the Lord took her home. Her parents who are dear friends of mine told me this story about Barbara and the angel who warned her not to return to her husband.

The angel my brother Jamie saw had wings. The one Barbara saw did not. He looked like an ordinary traveller.

2. Do angels have names?

Why shouldn't they have names? If God did not have names for His angels, He would be less efficient than Adam. Genesis 2:20 tells us *"...Adam gave names to all cattle, and to the fowl of the air, and to every beast of the field;..."*

God even has names for all the stars. Psalm 147:4, *"He telleth the number of the stars; he calleth them all by their names."* Some of their names are given to us in the Bible. (Job 9:9, Amos 5:8)

Yes, I believe that God who knows the numbers of the hairs of your head, and who sees when a sparrow falls, certainly has honoured the angels whom He has created and loves by giving them names. How else could He have order? He would never call them by a number. They are not prisoners.

3. What do the angels do?

This has already been discussed in detail but an outline review would be good here.

A. Angels were created to worship God. They know far better than we do His greatness, goodness and majesty. God never becomes commonplace to them. They are always filled with awe, reverence, respect, wonder and praise in His presence.

B. Angels were created to serve. They serve the Father, the Son and the Holy Spirit, always carrying out His orders. They also were created to serve us who are the heirs of salvation (Hebrews 1:14).

C. Many of the angels are warring angels, constantly engaged in warfare against the devil and the evil spirits.

D. Messenger angels are angels who have the task of delivering messages from one end of Heaven to the other and also from Heaven to earth and earth to Heaven.

E. Reporting angels are the angels that keep the records of every person who has ever lived. The files of Heaven are very accurate and always up to date and in order. They could produce the folio of your life instantly.

F. Musician angels are those who specialize in the choirs of Heaven and play all manner of instruments. They love to be with us when we sing and praise the Lord.

G. Guardian angels are those whose duty is to protect us. Psalm 91:11-12, *"For he shall give his angels charge over thee, to keep thee in all thy ways. They shall bear thee up in their hands, lest thou dash thy foot against a stone."* They keep us from falling, breaking our bones, all manner of accidents and help us to not get lost when we are travelling. I always ask God to send angels to protect me as I journey and I can give glory to God for His great protection in the millions of miles that I have travelled in over a hundred nations of the world in every means of conveyance imaginable. He has also protected me from fiery serpents, poisonous spiders and centipedes, scorpions and rats, wild beasts, mob violence as well as evil spirits and malicious and evil men (who are more wicked and to be feared even than all the above). I believe that I must really keep my angels busy!

When Daniel was cast into the lions' den, God sent His angel and shut the lions' mouths, so that they could not hurt Daniel (Daniel 6:22). That is supernatural protection. The lions had to recognize the commanding power of the angel.

H. Guiding angels. God has sent angels to guide His people to do the right thing and go the right way. God said to Moses, *"Behold, I send an angel before thee, to keep thee in the way, and to bring thee into the place which I have prepared."* (Exodus 23:20) Then God warned the Children of Israel that they must obey that guiding angel. *"Beware*

60

of him, and obey his voice, provoke him not; for he will not pardon your transgressions: for my name is in him. But if thou shalt indeed obey his voice, and do all that I speak; then I will be an enemy unto thine enemies, and an adversary unto thine adversaries.'' (Verses 21, 22)

Angels gave guidance to Hagar (Genesis 16:7-9), Lot (Genesis 19:15-20), Eliezer (Genesis 24:40), Jacob (Genesis 31:11), Gideon (Judges 6:11-14), Samson's parents (Judges 13:3, 13, 14), Joseph (Matthew 1:20, 2:13, 19), Mary Magdalene (Matthew 28:7), the Shepherds (Luke 2:9-12), Philip (Acts 8:26), Peter (Acts 10:3) and Paul (Acts 27:23-24).

4. How big are angels?

It seems that angels are many different sizes. Some have seen angels that are very small angels, others, whom I know, have seen average size (like an adult human), while still others have seen angels that are very large.

I had a missionary friend, Maxine, in Hong Kong who told me a wonderful testimony. Before she and her family came to work in Hong Kong, they ministered in Japan. Their home was near a canal. Maxine often had to leave her family alone at home while she went out to do missionary work for a few hours. Because of the close proximity of the canal to the house she was very worried that her young child could slip away from the servant, undetected, and fall into the canal. It troubled her so much that she couldn't keep her mind on her work.

One day she asked God for help and peace of mind. As she was praying, she was given a vision. She saw a huge angel, bigger than the house, standing guard. This greatly relieved her. After that she knew God was in control.

Whether or not angels are as big as a house I don't know,

61

but I do know God was showing my friend that God's keeping power and protecting power was big enough for any situation.

5. What kind of bodies do angels have?

God has created bodies for the angels which greatly resemble our resurrection bodies. They are not physical. They cannot feel pain, nor can swords nor bullets nor anything kill them. They are known to have eaten earthly food — Abraham fed the angels: *"And Abraham ran unto the herd and fetched a calf tender and good, and gave it unto a young man; and he hasted to dress it. And he took butter, and milk, and the calf which he had dressed, and set it before them; and he stood by them under the tree, and they did eat."* (Genesis 18:7, 8; also Genesis 19:3)

The manna which the children of Israel ate in the wilderness was called angel food Psalm 78:25: *"Man did eat angels' food:..."*

Angels can go through walls and doors. Nothing can stop them, they are unafraid of man or devil. They are never hindered by pain or physical weakness and they never tire to our knowledge.

They have no soulish desires, nor are they motivated by personal ambition, desire for wealth, the love of money, the comforts of life, the praises of man, the glory of fame nor sexual desires. The things that cause great men and women to fall into sin never will have any effect on the angels who stood the test in Heaven and stayed loyal and faithful to God.

Their appearance varied according to circumstances, but was often bright and dazzling (Matthew 28:2-7, Revelation 10:1,2).

6. What are the attributes and characteristics of the angels?

A. **Love**. The angels have perfect love. This love enables them to carry out the most difficult tasks. They have the true agape love. This is the unconditional love which flows from the heart of God and is available to all of us.

B. **Humility**. It is only through great humility that these wonderful, heavenly beings can serve man who is made lower than the angels (Psalm 8:5). In this they are like their Master, Jesus, who made Himself of no reputation (emptied Himself out) and took upon Him the form of a servant (*doulos*, i.e. "a slave") and was made in the likeness of men. *"But made himself of no reputation, and took upon him the form of a servant, and was made in the likeness of men: And being found in fashion as a man, he humbled himself, and became obedient unto death, even the death of the cross."* (Philippians 2:7, 8)

This humility is the trademark of every great saint. It does not only belong to the angel-band.

C. **Obedience**. This great attribute the angels undoubtedly also received by observing their Master, Jesus. They instantly obey the Lord. There is never any argument or disagreement or "back talk" which is so prevalent among God's children. How slow we are to obey! And how we love to argue, scheme and complain and make excuses when God asks us to do anything.

D. **Faithfulness**. The angels are faithful to God and to their charges. They can be trusted to do their best at all times.

E. **Loyalty**. Loyalty is becoming more and more a precious and rare trait. Distrust, strife, division and splits are the result of disloyalty which is treason in the camp. God is calling His anointed ones to be loyal to Him and to each other.

F. **Patience**. Oh, the wonderful patience of God's angels! They are long-suffering, forgiving again and again. They "find us in the Spirit" and this gives them a deep understanding of us which lends them patience.

We see their patience in their dealings with Lot and his wife. The angels tried to deliver them from the condemned city of Sodom, but Lot and his wife procrastinated, wasting precious moments away, while the angels, with great patience, still sought to hurry them up. They waited patiently until Lot, his wife and two younger daughters were out of the city before the fire and brimstone destroyed the city. But they could not save Lot's wife. She was turned into a pillar of salt when she looked back. It was not their fault. They had warned Lot and his family, *"...Escape for thy life; look not behind thee, neither stay thou in all the plain; escape to the mountain, lest thou be consumed..."* (Genesis 19:17-26) The angels can only protect us when we obey God. Disobedience takes the covering and protection off us.

I'm sure there are other attributes which you can discover. But these will suffice us for now.

7. Who is "the Angel of the Lord"?

In the Old Testament, there were certain times when a supernatural Being visited the earth and communicated with man. This Being undoubtedly is of higher rank than angels. For example in Exodus 3:2-4, the "Angel of the Lord" that spoke to Moses out of the midst of the bush was none other than the Lord Himself. (See Acts 7:30-38). I believe that this was God manifesting Himself to man in a special form and hence was none other than Christ's visible form before the incarnation. (Also see Genesis 18:2, 22 and Genesis 32:24, 30, 35:13-15).

8. Why do angels sometimes speak as though it is God speaking? For example they speak in the first person (e.g. Genesis 22:12, 16-19).

I believe that God is able to speak to man both audibly and in a way that only the spirit of man hears and not his natural ears. But still God often uses men and angels as His "mouthpiece." For example, the prophets spoke in the name of the Lord, using the first person. Although it is the voice of the prophet we hear or his hand that wrote it, still the message is from God. The prophet is only the instrument (Hebrews 1:1). So it was with angels also. They spoke in the first person, not because they were God, but because God spoke through them.

9. Why are Christians afraid of the subject of angels?

Satan has been very successful at putting a fear of the miraculous in the hearts of God's children. The Church, during the dark ages, fell so far away from the power and the scriptural understanding that the early church had that it lost many of our God-given truths, signs and miracles. For example, we lost even the fundamental truth of salvation by grace through faith (Ephesians 2:8). This is the very foundation of the Christian faith. If we could lose that, is it any wonder we lost the power of God, the truth of the precious Blood, the gifts of healing, miracles, discernment, the power to cast out demons, the gifts of prophecy, the truth of the evidence of speaking in tongues, and the ministry of angels.

Many of us remember being taught against the gift and evidence of speaking in tongues. We were even told that healing was of the devil. Is it any wonder the church became like the Sadducees who didn't believe in the miraculous (Acts

23:8) because they had lost the power and presence of God in their lives? *"Ye do err, not knowing the Scriptures, nor the power of God."* (Matthew 22:29) People are afraid of anything that their small minds can't understand. And without the Holy Spirit to teach our minds, our understanding is limited. Some of God's people will even be afraid of this book. Yet they will let the devil use them and obey demons. They need not to fear the devil, but fear God instead (Matthew 10:28). We are taught to fear the wrong things. Instead of fearing sin and evil, we fear the good angels who try to keep us from sin, evil and hell.

10. What gender are angels, male or female?

Jesus answered this question when He spoke about married life in Heaven (Matthew 22:30; read the verses 23-29 which precede this verse, Mark 12:24-25 and Luke 20:34-36.)

Angels have bodies which have never lost the glory, like ours did through sin. They were never given the ability to procreate. Therefore they have no sexual organs at all. They are neither male nor female. But they can have the features of a strong man or the more delicate features of a woman. God is a God of variety. He never creates clones. Just as every person is different and every finger-print and snowflake has its individual design, so every angel has his own personality, form, appearance, features and shape. They were created according to God's will and plan.

11. Are angels still being created?

I do not know the answer to this question. Certainly, God who can do anything is able to create more angels if He needs them. But I think He is training His saints who have "graduated" from this earth to do many of the heavenly tasks.

As we are promoted to glory, we can perform many of the duties of angels, thus freeing the angels to do other work. If we will one day be equal to angels (Luke 20:36), what hinders God from giving us angel assignments when we are ready for that higher plane of service?

12. What language do angels speak?

I believe they speak any language they need to speak. In the Old Testament when they communicated with man, they spoke the language of the person with whom they talked. In most cases it was Hebrew. But Balaam wasn't an Israelite and so the angel who stopped him on the road would have spoken his language (Numbers 22:32). Peter probably spoke Aramaic. So the angel would have used the Aramaic tongue.

Cornelius was a Roman, so the angel who told him to call for Peter to come to his house would likely have spoken Latin or Greek (Acts 10:3, 7, 22).

In the mission fields where I have worked, the different people who have seen angels and heard them speak have always heard them speak in their own language.

13. What is the "tongue of angels" mentioned in I Corinthians 13:1, "Though I speak with the tongues of men and of angels, and have not charity, I am become as sounding brass, or a tinkling cymbal."?

The "tongues" of angels undoubtedly refers to the languages of Heaven. Some think it is Hebrew, but the Bible never tells us what it is.

14. What does Paul mean by Colossians 2:18: "Let no man beguile you of your reward in a voluntary humility and worshipping of angels, intruding into those things which

he hath not seen vainly puffed up by his fleshly mind.''?

God does not want us to worship any other being than the Lord Himself. The word "worship" here means "an outward act of ceremony and adoration."

While we can respect and love angels just like we respect and love a true friend, we must never worship an angel any more than we should worship a friend. Adoration of any created being is a sin. Our adoration belongs to God alone.

God said to Moses and the children of Israel, *"Thou shalt have no other gods before me. Thou shalt not make unto thee any graven image, or any likeness of any thing that is in heaven above, or that is in the earth beneath, or that is in the water under the earth. Thou shalt not bow down thyself to them, nor serve them: for I the Lord thy God am a jealous God,…"* (Exodus 20:3-5)

It is wrong to bow in worship before angels, saints or images of saints or any other object of worship other than God. We must never bow to worship before anyone but the Lord.

In Revelation 22:8, 9 when John had finished receiving the great end-time revelation, he *"fell down to worship before the feet of the angel which showed him these things."* But the angel said to him: *…See thou do it not: for I am thy fellow servant, and of thy brethren the prophets, and of them which keep the sayings of this book: worship God."*

Apparently this heavenly being was not an angel as we understand angels to be but a glorified being, probably an Old Testament saint who never let his identity be known, but he was permitted to come to earth, even to the isle of Patmos and give John these great revelations. He knew the future, just like Moses and Elijah did when they, too, were permitted to come to earth and commune with Jesus on the Mount of

Transfiguration and talk about *"...his decease which he should accomplish at Jerusalem."* (Luke 9:31)

God reserves all worship for Himself and His Son alone. Therefore it is wrong to worship angels.

15. Do angels sing?

Of course, angels sing. In Job 38 we read that wonderful account of God telling Job and his companions the glorious story of creation. In verses 4-7 he asks Job, *"Where wast thou...When the morning stars sang together, and all the sons of God shouted for joy?"*

We know that the stars refers to angels (Revelation 12:4) So God was simply remembering the beautiful music of the great angel choirs that sang the first magnificent creation oratorio. Franz Joseph Haydn, when he composed *Die Schoepfung* (The Creation) in 1798, may have been permitted to hear this original angelic music of the Creation. In Luke 2:13, 14 we read about another great oratorio of praise. This was the oratorio of the Incarnation of the Son of God. *"And suddenly there was with the angel a multitude of the heavenly host praising God, and saying, Glory to God in the highest, and on earth peace, good will toward men."* People will wish to argue that the angels did not sing. But this is only because they are limited in their understanding of the word "praising." This word is *aineo* which means "to **sing** alternately praises to God." It comes from the word *ainos*, which means "to praise for benefits received."

One time I was standing in the Garden Tomb in Jerusalem with members of our tour group. In those days the crowds who visited the Garden Tomb were not so large so one could spend considerable time there. While we were praising God, I "heard" in the Spirit the angel choirs singing the

Resurrection Anthem of praise which they sang on the morning of the resurrection. It is not recorded in the Scripture, but I heard their song of praise and victory and no one can make me believe otherwise.

16. What did the writer of Hebrews mean by "Be not forgetful to entertain strangers: for thereby some have entertained angels unawares." (Hebrews 13:2)?

It is obvious that angels have the ability to hide their identity so that they are not recognized. This was true of Manoah as well as others both in the Bible and out of the Bible. We would certainly be very courteous if an angel visited us. The Lord wants us to be kind and gracious to all strangers, for there is a possibility that we will be rewarded by an "angel visit" and not even know it until it's too late.

STUDY QUESTIONS

1. Explain what different types of angels there are and what their different ministries are.

2. Memorize Psalm 91:11-12.

3. Give six different characteristics of the angels.

4. Who is the Angel of the Lord?

5. Explain what the word "praise" really means in the Greek.

CHAPTER NINE

INTERESTING ANGEL STORIES
IN THE OLD TESTAMENT

The Old Testament is full of many interesting stories about angels. Sometimes it was the great ones who were visited by angels and sometimes it was the unknown, least expected who were honoured by the visitation of an angel. But one thing is certain: it usually was a life-changing experience. People were never the same again. It is impossible at this time to reiterate every one of the angel stories told in the Bible. If you want to study about each of them, you can do research with a good concordance and Bible dictionary. But let us begin with Abraham.

1. Abraham

Abraham had more than one encounter with angels. When he camped in the plains of Mamre, he was visited one day by what appears to have been the pre-incarnate Christ who was accompanied by two angels (Genesis 18:1-33). I love the way he washed their feet and invited them to rest in the shade of the tree, just like one would for a mortal in the heat of the day. Then he asked Sarah to prepare cakes with the finest of meal while he himself ran out to the herd to select a special fatted calf which one of the servants butchered. He then proceeded to cook it. When it was ready, he "set the table" with the freshly baked bread, butter and calf-stew. That together made a tasty meal. The Lord ate and the angels enjoyed their meal which they ate under the tree. Obviously, neither the Lord nor the angels were vegetarians! When Jesus was still on earth, after His resurrection, He ate broiled fish (Luke 24:41-42).

Later that day, Abraham interceded for the city of Sodom and for Lot, his nephew. It was probably these two angels who visited Sodom and brought out Lot and his family.

Some years later, God tested Abraham's obedience and love when He asked him to offer up his son Isaac as a sacrifice on Mt. Moriah (Genesis 22). Abraham, with a broken heart, raised his knife to slay Isaac when the Angel of the Lord called to him out of Heaven and stopped him. It had only been a test. I'm sure that must have been one of the most wonderful messages the angels have ever brought to man. It was a thing that concerned them very much, because earlier the angels had brought the wonderful news that one year after their first visit Sarah would bear Abraham a son. In the same way that we would have a special attachment to any child whose birth we had prophesied, the angels must have had a special interest in Isaac and a very special love for him.

Some years ago I was visiting a friend in the hospital who was in danger of having a miscarriage. I had been preaching in their church. On Sunday afternoon, her husband, Rev. Robert Doorn, took me to the hospital to visit his wife Glenyce. Because of hemorrhaging, her condition was very negative. Suddenly, as I laid hands on her and prayed for her, the Spirit of God came on me and I began to prophesy, "Fear not, for thou shalt have this child also, and she shall be My handmaiden, for I have called her from the womb to serve Me." After the words came out of my mouth and I realized I had said that it would be a daughter (they had two sons), I was shocked but confident that it was God. Glenyce recovered and carried the baby to full term. The doctor and nurses both warned them that they must not set their hopes too high because from every indication and their many years of experience they were positively sure it was a boy.

The day of delivery came. As Glenyce was in labour, again the doctor and nurse tried to prepare them for a son, but they said, "No, it's a girl. God told Sister Gwen, it's a girl, and it is a girl! You will see!" The doctor and nurse could only shake their heads. When the baby arrived, IT WAS A GIRL! A beautiful, healthy girl. They called her Susan.

What about me? I confess I was happy for my friends and relieved to know she was what God had promised and was healthy. Now she is a lovely lassie, fourteen years old. There is a special relationship of the Lord between us. I know it is because of the Word of the Lord God gave me for her when she still was only a tiny foetus in the uterus of her mother.

2. Jacob

Jacob's first visitation (Genesis 29:12-16): Jacob, the twin son of Isaac and Rebecca had more than one remarkable visitation of angels. The first one was on the night that he fled from the face of his angry brother Esau after deceiving his father and thus obtaining Esau's blessing for himself. As he lay down in the open field to sleep, he had a dream that was filled with angelic activity. *"And he dreamed, and behold a ladder set up on the earth, and the top of it reached to heaven: and behold the angels of God ascending and descending on it. And, behold, the Lord stood above it, and said, I am the Lord God of Abraham thy father, and the God of Isaac: the land whereon thou liest, to thee will I give it,*

*and to thy seed; And thy seed shall be as the dust of the earth;
and thou shalt spread abroad to the west, and to the east,
and to the north, and to the south: and in thee and in thy
seed shall all the families of the earth be blessed. And, behold,
I am with thee, and will keep thee in all places whither thou
goest, and will bring thee again into this land; for I will not
leave thee, until I have done that which I have spoke to thee
of.''*

Angels always accompany the messages we receive from
Heaven. These angels who heard God's promises to Jacob
would later become helpers of the children of Jacob (Israel)
through the centuries to follow. They would help to deliver
them from Egypt, fight with them against the Canaanites,
and later their other enemies, deliver them from Babylon,
help them overcome their enemies and finally, even today,
they are the everlasting angels who fight Israel's battles, and
will lead them back to Israel from the nations of the diaspora.

b. His second visitation (Genesis 32:24-29): Another
very important visit Jacob had with angels was that night at
Peniel when he prepared his heart to meet his angry brother
Esau who was coming after him with four hundred men. In
great fear and trembling he sent costly gifts of cattle and sheep
ahead of him as presents to Esau while he stayed alone on
the other side of the brook of Jabbok where an angel of the
Lord met him and wrestled with him until daybreak. With
terrible, desperate strength Jacob wrestled with his heavenly
opponent. And finally, when the morning was breaking, and
the angel knew he had to return, he touched (*naga*, "to strike")
the hollow of Jacob's thigh, causing it to come out of joint.
Still, in spite of the terrible pain, Jacob hung on, struggling
desperately and crying out, *"...I will not let thee go, except
thou bless me."* (Genesis 32:26)

The angel had the authority to change Jacob's name to Israel, "Prince," and he also changed Jacob's nature and broke his cunning and scheming spirit. He could never have become the Prince of Israel if God had not broken his spirit. Neither can we be what God wants us to be unless our stubborn, rebellious, tricky, scheming, selfish and self-preserving spirits are broken before God. Some of us need a one-night wrestling match with the Angel of God that is born out of an honest appraisal of our helpless situation.

Our "Esaus" are on their way to meet us. "Pay-day" is due and we won't be ready to meet our foe, unless we have prayed through in the night-time of our soul.

3. Balaam (Numbers 22)

The Word of God clearly states *"But they that will be rich fall into temptation and a snare, and into many foolish and hurtful lusts, which drown men in destruction and perdition. For the love of money is the root of all evil: which while some coveted after, they have erred from the faith, and pierced themselves through with many sorrows."* (I Timothy 6:9, 10)

If a man does not have a true foundation, he is easily tempted to seek and appreciate earthly gain more than spiritual rewards.

Balaam fell because of the great rewards of fame, position and money which Balak, the Moabitish king offered him if he would come and work divination against Israel in a way that would destroy them.

God clearly said, *"Thou shalt not go with them; thou shalt not curse the people: for they are blessed."* (Numbers 22:12) But when Balak offered great rewards and sent greater ambassadors to beg him to come and they told Balaam that Balak had sent a message saying, *"...Let nothing, I pray thee, hinder thee from coming unto me: For I will promote thee unto very great honour, and I will do whatsoever thou sayest unto me: come therefore, I pray thee, curse me this people."* (Verses 16 and 17) Balaam was tempted, so that night God let him have his own way.

God has made us a free moral agent. We can do what we want. He warns us, He sends prophets and gives us dreams and speaks through His Word and by showing us signs of His will, but if we want to disregard His warning, He lets us go our way.

However, because of God's love for Israel, He sent an angel to stop Balaam. The Bible says, *"And Balaam rose up in the morning, and saddled his ass, and went with the princes of Moab. And God's anger was kindled because he went: and the angel of the Lord stood in the way for an adversary against him. Now he was riding upon his ass, and his two servants were with him. And the ass saw the angel of the Lord standing in the way, and his sword drawn in his hand: and the ass turned aside out of the way, and went into the field: and Balaam smote the ass, to turn her into the way."* (Numbers 22:21-23)

Balaam was so angry at his ass, that he would have killed it if he had had a sword. The ass saw what Balaam didn't see. When the ass spoke to him and God opened his eyes to see, he realized that the ass had seen the angel and that was why he had refused to go farther. Furthermore, the angel said that he had stopped him, *"...because thy way is perverse before me."* (Verse 32) And then he added that if the ass had not turned aside three times, he would have killed Balaam, but saved the ass.

Why is it so hard for men to hear the voice of God and to know His will? Why are animals more able to know God and sometimes hear His voice better than man? It is a tragic thing when a dumb ass can see God and a prophet doesn't. The money and the rewards had blinded the eyes of Balaam. When he offered to turn back, the angel let him go because he knew the weakness of the man and that he would always be influenced at another time to "curse for gain."

In my life, I have seen many sell out their call for earthly gain. I have seen them plot, plan and scheme to do what they want to do and yet still make it appear as if they are doing God's will. Neither the voice of God nor an angel of the Lord can stop them. They are those who Peter (II Peter 2:15), and Jude (verse 11) and John (Revelation 2:14) called false prophets who have sold out their souls for earthly gain and shall perish in shame.

The angel, who stopped Balaam temporarily, could have been Michael because he was guardian of Israel. Balaam was not permitted to curse Israel. He came to curse, but stayed to bless. But in the end, he taught the Moabites how to cause Israel to fall into the sin of adultery and idolatry so that God Himself smote them and 24,000 died of a plague which Bible historians believe was an outbreak of sexually transmitted diseases (Numbers 25:9).

God can send angels to warn us and try to stop us, but when we still insist on doing our own will, God lets us. But in the end it is to our destruction. Be careful therefore that you obey the angel of the Lord who has been sent to guide you.

4. Gideon (Judges 6)

Gideon, the son of Joash, of the tribe of Manasseh, received his call to lead the children of Israel to warfare against the Midianites through an angel. It might have been the same angel as the one who met Balaam. Gideon had a long conversation with the angel (Judges 6:11-24). He not only received his call, he also got the answer to some questions that were on his heart. Then he prepared a meal for the angel. No doubt he had learned this from the story of Abraham. But this time the angel did not eat the food. Instead, he touched the food with his staff, whereupon there rose up fire out of the rock which consumed the flesh and the cakes. When the angel left him, Gideon was overwrought because now he was convinced his visitor had been an angel of the Lord and he would die. But God spoke to him, *"...Peace be unto thee; fear not: for thou shalt not die."* Then Gideon built an altar there unto the Lord and called it Jehovah-Shalom (the Lord is my peace).

It is only when you have the deep peace of God in your heart that God can use you to do great things for Him. You can never lead others to victory if you do not have *Shalom*, the Prince of Peace in your heart.

5. Samson (Judges 13)

Samson, of the tribe of Dan, received his call even before he was conceived in his mother's womb through a visitation of an angel to his mother (Judges 13:3-7). When she told her husband Manoah about it, he also wanted to see the angel. Josephus, the historian, says that he was very jealous. Anyway, the angel came the second time and the woman ran to call her husband. After a lengthy conversation in which the angel repeated everything he had said to Manoah's wife, Manoah offered food to the angel who also offered it up as a burnt offering to God, for he said, *"...if thou wilt offer a burnt offering, thou must offer it unto the Lord."* (Judges 13:16) When Manoah asked the angel what his name was, the angel said, *"...Why askest thou thus after my name, seeing it is a secret?"* (Verse 18) This word "secret" is *pilly* or *pally,* which means, "incomprehensible, wonderful, remarkable, supernatural." Sometimes the wonders of God and His supernatural acts are so wonderful that they remain a secret to our natural, carnal understanding.

6. David (II Samuel 24, I Chronicles 21)

God usually spoke to David through His prophets Samuel, Nathan and Gad. It was near the end of his life, after he had committed his sin of numbering the people and God had sent judgment through a terrible pestilence which broke out upon Israel, causing the death of 70,000 from Dan to Beersheba in one day, that David saw the first angel recorded in his life.

The angel of judgment was taking a tithe of the men of war. God was angry with David because he had, out of pride, committed an act of disobedience and started counting the people. God knew his heart.

It was only after the angel began smiting the people of Jerusalem that David lifted up his eyes, and saw the angel of the Lord stand between the earth and the Heaven. The angel had the drawn sword in his hand and it was stretched out over Jerusalem. David (and the elders of Jerusalem who were already clothed in sackcloth) cried to God for mercy and he took the blame upon himself. Through his intercession, humility and confession he obtained mercy from God. (I Chronicles 21:15-17)

It's a terrible thing when our sins cause the angel of wrath to draw his sword against us or those whom we love.

7. Elijah (I Kings 19:1-8)

Angels visited Elijah more than once; however, I would only like to share one incident of angelic visitation in his life. This took place after Elijah had called down fire at Mt. Carmel and was on his way into the wilderness, fleeing for his life from the wrathful Jezebel who had threatened to kill him.

Weary and exhausted from running without food, he fell down under a juniper tree in the wilderness and begged God to take his life.

Human nature can be ridiculous. If he wanted to die that badly, why was he running from Jezebel? But God understood his heart. God granted his heart's desire, not his cry of desperation that came out of exhaustion and weariness of the soul.

While he slept, an angel came and baked him a cake on coals of fire (probably fresh from off the heavenly altar). When it was ready, the angel touched him gently and awakened him, bidding him to arise and eat. When Elijah saw the hot bread (who doesn't like hot, fresh bread) and a cruise of water, he ate and drank, and then promptly lay back down and fell asleep again.

The second time the angel touched him and, waking him, said, *"Arise and eat because the journey is too great for thee."* (Verse 7) And he arose and ate some more and went in the strength of that food forty days and forty nights unto Horeb, the Mountain of God where God gave him three great revelations.

We may never have the privilege of having angels visit us, giving us angel food, but we can eat the manna of the Word of God which was delivered to us by angels (Hebrews 2:2) and receive strength from God's Word for the great journey of life that lies before us.

Never neglect to eat "angel food," even the Word of God, every morning before you begin your day's journey. You will need it before the day is out because there are many "Jezebel demons" out there waiting to destroy you and rob you of your life's calling. Always remember the words of the angel, *"...Arise and eat; because the journey is too great for thee."* (I Kings 19:7)

8. Elisha

A beautiful and humorous story is told in II Kings 6:5-23 of how the king of Syria sent a great host with horses and chariots to Dothan to capture Elisha who was giving the King of Israel secret intelligence about every military move Syria was planning (II Kings 6:12). When his servant saw this great host, he was full of fear and cried, *"...Alas, my master! how shall we do?"*

Elisha answered him, *"...Fear not: for they that be with us are more than they that be with them."*

Then Elisha asked God to open the eyes of his servant, so he would see the heavenly hosts which Elisha was seeing. The lord opened his eyes and he saw the mountain was full of horses and fire round about Elisha.

Then Elisha asked God to smite the Syrian soldiers with blindness and Elisha led those blinded men straight into Samaria where they were taken captive by Israel.

b. II Kings 7:1-20: The angel hosts chase an army.

81

Another humorous story is told of how four lepers left the besieged city of Samaria to try to get food from the enemy because they were starving to death. When they arrived at the camp of the Syrians there wasn't a soul in the camp. They had heard an approaching "army" that had terrified them and they had fled in terror, leaving all their supplies behind and a trail of garments and vessels which they cast away in their haste. I believe it was the angel hosts that had chased them.

9. Jehoshaphat's Angelic Helpers

There is one more war story I want to tell you about. It is in II Chronicles 20. When Jehoshaphat led his people to battle, they were defenceless against an army much greater than themselves. But as they obeyed the word of the prophet and began to sing and praise the Lord, a wonderful thing happened: the Lord sent ambushments against the enemy, and they destroyed each other (II Chronicles 20:22).

When we sing and praise the Lord in the middle of our trials and testings, it attracts the angels because they love our praises. They will be drawn to come to us and defend and help us when we praise more than when we beg or complain about a situation.

How did these ambushments accomplish such a great victory? They intermingled themselves among the enemy hosts. Because they were unseen when they struck out at one of the soldiers, when he turned to see who had struck him, he only saw his fellow soldier. But because he was so angry, he did not stop to reason, so without reasoning he pulled out his sword and struck back at his comrade who he thought had hit him. In a minute they were fighting each other. The Bible says that this happened throughout the camp of the enemy. *"For the children of Ammon and Moab stood up against the inhabitants of mount Seir, utterly to slay and destroy them: and when they had made an end of the inhabitants of Seir, every one helped to destroy another."* (II Chronicles 20:23) When the children of Israel arrived on the battle scene, there wasn't one soul left alive.

The evil spirits do the same thing among the Christians. They post themselves between two Christians and give off their evil vibrations, causing God's people to feel that they are receiving this "hate" feeling from each other rather than from its real source. Soon this causes distrust, suspicion, anger, retaliation and even fights among God's people which bring about splits and divisions. Satan has nothing new. He only copies that which God does. He saw God used ambushments, so he uses them, too. Sometimes they are not only demons, but demon-possessed or demon-controlled people who will let the devil use them. Even Christians are guilty of this error.

10. Post-Babylonic Angelic Ministry

The angels undoubtedly accompanied the Children of Israel on their return from exile. Ezra in Ezra 8:21-32 tells how he was ashamed to ask the king for a band of soldiers to protect him and his band of returning exiles on that long five months journey from Babylon to Jerusalem. Instead, he went to God for help and proclaimed a fast at the river of Ahava, to seek for God's help for them on that long journey. Remember, Zerubbabel had brought only men back to Jerusalem. Ezra was bringing women and children (Ezra 8:21) and the precious vessels from the sanctuary which were worth millions. The road was full of robbers and bandits who lay

83

in wait for just such a treasure-trove to come through. Without God's help they would never have made it. But the Lord brought them safely to their destination without a single loss. Fasting brings angelic help and protection in dangerous situations. When the enemy comes against you, find an "Ahava" place in your life where you can seek the face of God in fasting and prayer so that you can win the victory and march through enemy infested, devil-territory unharmed.

11. Zechariah

Zechariah's remarkable end-time prophecy was given almost entirely through angels speaking to Zechariah and showing him things to come, even things which concern Israel in these end-times.

STUDY QUESTIONS

1. What were Jacob's two encounters with angels and how did it affect his life?

2. How did David obtain mercy from God?

3. How did God intervene on Jehoshaphat's behalf?

4. In what way does Satan copy this?

5. What will help us to get angelic help when Satan launches an attack against us?

CHAPTER TEN

PROPHETIC VISITATIONS
IN THE NEW TESTAMENT

The New Testament was ushered in by the ministry of angels.

1. Gabriel Appears to Zacharias (Luke 1:5-25)

Zacharias, the priest from the tribe of Levi whose wife was Elisabeth, a cousin of Mary's, was ministering in the temple of Jerusalem, performing his priestly duties, when the Archangel Gabriel appeared unto him suddenly. The angel stood on the right side of the altar of incense in the holy place. This was one of the three pieces of furniture in the holy place. There was, besides this one, the table of shewbread, and the candlestick. The altar of incense was a type of the prayers of the saints and the sweet fragrance of the Lord. The instant Zacharias saw him, he was struck with fear. But Gabriel said to him, *"...Fear not, Zacharias: for thy prayer is heard; and thy wife Elisabeth shall bear thee a son, and thou shalt call his name John. And thou shalt have joy and gladness; and many shall rejoice at his birth. For he shall be great in the sight of the Lord, and shall drink neither wine nor strong drink; and he shall be filled with the Holy Ghost, even from his mother's womb. And many of the children of Israel shall he turn to the Lord their God. And he shall go before him in the spirit and power of Elijah, to turn the hearts of the fathers to the children, and the disobedient to the wisdom*

of the just; to make ready a people prepared for the Lord."
(Luke 1:13-17)

Zacharias not only had fear; he also had unbelief. Usually these two go together. He asked for a sign: *"Whereby shall I know this?"* (In other words, "what proof can you give me?") *"...I am an old man and my wife well stricken in years."*

Now Zacharias and Elisabeth were *"...both righteous before God, walking in all the commandments and ordinances of the Lord blameless."* (Luke 1:6) They had never had any children. The Bible says Elisabeth was barren. By this time they had given up all hope of having a child. It is no wonder that Zacharias found it hard to believe, but God nevertheless was displeased with his unbelief for without faith it is impossible to please God (Hebrews 11:6). When he asked for a sign, Gabriel was displeased with him. He gave him a sign, but it was not a good sign. Gabriel said, *"...I am Gabriel, that stand in the presence of God; and am sent to speak unto thee, and to show thee these glad tidings. And, behold, thou shalt be dumb, and not able to speak, until the day that these things shall be performed, because thou believest not my words, which shall be fulfilled in their season."* (Luke 1:19, 20)

When Zacharias came out of the holy place, *"...he could not speak unto them: and they perceived that he had seen a vision in the temple; for he beckoned unto them, and remained speechless."* (Verse 22) When his duties were fulfilled in the temple, he returned to his village and Elizabeth conceived, even as Gabriel had said.

It was the month of Tammuz. We know this because the course is mentioned under which he served. *"There was in the days of Herod, the king of Judea, a certain priest named Zacharias, of the course Abijah:..."* (Luke 1:5) I Chronicles

24:10 tells us that this course was the 8th of 24. We know from the history of Jewish religion and tradition that this course of Abijah was in the month of Tammuz which is the same as our late June and early July. So Elisabeth would have likely conceived in the early part of July.

2. The Angel Gabriel Appears to the Virgin Mary in Nazareth (Luke 1:26-27):

One of the most beautiful stories in the world is found between verses 26-37 of Luke 1. The gentleness of the great Angel Gabriel with this little maid is so noticeable. He greets her with words of great honour, *"...Hail, thou that art highly favoured, the Lord is with thee: blessed art thou among women."* (Luke 1:28)

When she was troubled and perplexed about all these fine words, he understood her and said, *"...Fear not, Mary: for thou hast found favour with God. And, behold, thou shalt conceive in thy womb, and bring forth a son, and shalt call his name Jesus. He shall be great, and shall be called the Son of the Highest; and the Lord God shall give unto him the throne of his father David: And he shall reign over the house of Jacob for ever; and of his kingdom there shall be no end."* (Luke 1:30-33) Mary asked him, *"...How shall this be, seeing I know not a man?"* (Verse 34) The word "know" is *ginosko* and means not only to know experientially and intuitively, but also have sexual relations.

By this we know that even though Mary was betrothed to Joseph, she was still a virgin. Gabriel then explained to her how this miraculous conception would take place: *"The Holy Ghost shall come upon thee, and the power of the Highest shall overshadow thee: therefore also that holy thing* which shall be born of thee shall be called the Son of God." (Luke 1:35) And then he told her, *"And, behold, thy cousin Elisabeth, she hath also conceived a son in her old age; and this is the sixth month with her, who was called barren."* (Verse 36)

We all know that six months after the month of Tammuz is the month of Tebeth which begins in our late December, early January. So, this was then when the annunciation took place. It must have happened immediately because Mary *"arose in those days, and went into the hill country with haste,..."* to visit Elisabeth. When she walked in the door, the Spirit of God fell on Elisabeth and she began to prophesy under the unction of the Holy Spirit, *"...Blessed art thou among women, and blessed is the fruit of thy womb. And whence is this to me, that the mother of my Lord should come to me?"* (Luke 1:42, 43) She said more, but suffice it to say, she recognized that Mary already was with child by the sovereign power of God. Add nine months to the last of December and the first part of January, and we have the end of September or the beginning of October, the approximate time of the Feast of Tabernacles which, according to Jewish tradition, was when they expected the Messiah to appear.

3. Joseph and the Angels

We already mentioned in Chapter Six how the angel appeared to Joseph in a dream twice. Altogether, there were three times: 1. Matthew 1:18-20, 2. Matthew 2:13, 3. Matthew 2:19, 20.

4. Angels in Bethlehem

It bears repeating here again how the angels visited the shepherds on the night that Jesus was born. Read carefully the beautiful story of Luke 2:1-20.

The angels and all Heaven rejoiced when Jesus was born. They knew He had come for one great purpose, that was to bring peace on earth and good will between all men and all nations. There would no more be a wall of partition between Jew and Gentile, bond and free, male and female. If we all would come to Christ, we would all be one. This would bring joy, harmony and peace. All these were a reality in Heaven and it was Heaven's desire, for this war-torn and bleeding planet with all the wars and hatred to be healed so that we may have Heaven on earth. Oh, God, thy Kingdom come!

5. Angels at the Scene of Crucifixion and Resurrection

We have already mentioned in Chapter Six how Jesus said He could have called the angels to deliver Him from the hands of those who wanted to crucify Him. We have described their presence at the tomb on the morning of the resurrection. All of the great happenings in the life of our Lord Jesus, from His conception to His ascension, were accompanied by the manifestation of angels.

6. Angels and the Church Age:

All through the Book of Acts, we see the ministry of the angels. They accompanied the apostles, spoke to them, delivered them, gave them messages from the Throne and I am sure that some day in Heaven, when we meet the early church saints who went through great fiery trials, they will tell us of how angels were with them to strengthen them (even like Jesus was strengthened in Gethsemane) and to accompany them to the arena where they died as martyrs. They will introduce the angels who were with them in the hour of their trial, for they will know them even like my brother Jamie, who said, "Gwen, I would recognize him anywhere."

Peter will say, "This is the angel who brought me out of prison the first time when I was imprisoned in Jerusalem (Acts 5:17-25) and the second time (Acts 12:1-19) Take time now to read these true accounts from your Bible and meditate on them and God will show you beautiful truths about the ministry of His angels to us.

7. Paul (Acts 27:13-44)

Paul, the great Apostle was often visited by the Lord and His angels during His time of service to God. One of the greatest stories takes place one night on the stormy seas of the Mediterranean as Paul is being brought, as a prisoner under guard, to Rome.

After many days on the sea, when all hope that they could be saved was lost, the Angel of the Lord stood beside Paul and said, *"...Fear not, Paul; thou must be brought before Caesar: and, lo, God hath given thee all them that sail with thee."* (Acts 27:24)

When you get a message like that from one of God's great angels, you are confident that it shall truly be even as it was told you. (Acts 27:25)

8. Philip and the Angel (Acts 8:26-40)

Here we see another wonderful happening. An Ethiopian government official is returning back to Ethiopia from Jerusalem on the great old Roman Road that reached from Israel through Egypt all the way to Ethiopia. He is reading the Book of Isaiah. His searching heart was longing to know the truth.

In that hour the angel of the Lord visited Philip who was in Samaria and commanded him, *"...Arise, and go toward the south unto the way that goeth down from Jerusalem unto Gaza, which is desert."* (Acts 9:26)

Philip was in the midst of a great revival in Samaria when the angel sent him "to the desert." It's a good thing he didn't have any advertisement out announcing his revival. He would have had a hard time breaking off his meetings! But, because he was under Holy Ghost appointment, he could come and go as the Spirit led him.

There on that highway, he "hitch-hiked" a ride with the grand chariot of the official from Ethiopia. Hearing the man of great importance reading the prophet Isaiah, he asked him, "Do you understand what you are reading?"

The eunuch answered him, "How can I without someone to teach me the meaning?" And then he invited Philip to come and sit beside him.

"What does this mean?" he asked, " *'He was led as a sheep to the slaughter; and like a lamb dumb before his shearer, so opened he not his mouth: In his humiliation his judgment was taken away: and who shall declare his generation? for his life is taken from the earth.? Who is the prophet talking about, himself or some other man?' "*

Then Philip opened his mouth and (taking this Scripture

91

as his text) preached unto him Jesus.

We know the rest of the story; the eunuch believed, Philip baptized him and he continued on his way to Ethiopia where he took the Gospel to his own people. Why did the angel have to send Philip into the desert to preach the Gospel? Why couldn't the angel have appeared personally to the official and explained the Scripture? Surely he knew that the 53rd chapter of Isaiah, from which he was reading, referred to the Messiah.

But again, we see that the angels were not permitted to preach the Gospel.

Why then did Paul warn the church of Galatians: *"But though we, or an angel from heaven, preach any other gospel unto you than that which we have preached unto you, let him be accursed."* (Galatians 1:8)?

While some Bible scholars believe that this statement was simply a hypothesis which has no basis for fact, still let us not forget that some of the world's religions and cults have been introduced by so-called "angels."

Mohammed said he received the Koran from an angel whom he called Gabriel. Joseph Smith claimed he received his instruction from an angel called Moroni who gave him "golden plates" which he translated into the Book of Mormon.

God's angels do not cross this line, but the fallen angels who appear as the good angels of light break this law.

9. Cornelius and the Angel

Angels never preach the Gospel. That is our task. We, redeemed sinners, who have been saved by grace have received the Great Commission. That is why, when the Roman military officer Cornelius who lived in Caesarea was seeking for the truth of God, the angel of the Lord told him to send his

92

servant to Joppa, where they would find a man by the name of Simon Peter who was living in the house of a tanner by the name of Simon who lived by the sea side. *"...he shall tell thee what thou oughtest to do."* (Acts 10:1-6)

Four days later when Peter arrived at the home of Cornelius, this great Roman officer told him what exactly had happened that had caused him to call for Peter: *"...Four days ago I was fasting until this hour; and at the ninth hour I prayed in my house, and behold, a man stood before me in bright clothing, And said, Cornelius, thy prayer is heard, and thine alms are had in remembrance in the sight of God. Send therefore to Joppa, and call hither Simon, whose surname is Peter; he is lodged in the house of one Simon a tanner by the sea side: who, when he cometh, shall speak unto thee. Immediately therefore I sent to thee; and thou hast well done that thou art come. Now therefore are we all here present before God, to hear all things that are commanded thee of God."* (Acts 10:30-33)

The remarkable part of this whole wonderful episode was that Cornelius and his acquaintances who heard Peter preach the Gospel were the first Gentiles in recorded Scripture to believe and receive the Holy Spirit. This was the first outpouring of the Holy Ghost on the Gentiles. I am sure this was the reason that the angel was divinely appointed to give Cornelius this high counsel to fetch Peter, even telling him Peter's address and the occupation of Peter's host, *"...one Simon a tanner, whose house is by the sea side:..."*

Why didn't the angel preach the Gospel to Cornelius? Had angels not attended Jesus' life from birth to ascension? It was because they only do that which God has created them to do. They do not break their ranks. Preaching the Gospel is our task.

STUDY QUESTIONS

1. What was Zacharias' sin that caused the angel to strike him with dumbness?

2. Explain why Jesus was most probably born in September or October.

3. At what three occasions did the angel appear to Joseph?

4. Why did the angel send Philip to the desert to preach to the eunuch instead of doing it himself?

5. Why does Paul warn of any angels preaching "any other gospel" (Galatians 1:8)?

CHAPTER ELEVEN

ANGELS IN THE BOOK OF REVELATION

John, the Beloved Revelator, and Angels

In the Book of Revelation, we find angels mentioned many times. The word "angel" in the singular is mentioned at least fifty times and the word "angels" about two dozen times.

The Book of Revelation is introduced in Chapter One, verse one with this introduction, *"The Revelation of Jesus Christ, which God gave unto him, to show unto his servants things which must shortly come to pass; and he sent and signified it by his angel unto his servant John."* We see it was an angel who knew the times and seasons, a special messenger who gave John the end-time prophetic revelations which he received. Daniel also received his end-time revelations through an angel.

Each of the seven churches mentioned in Revelation, Chapters Two and Three had a guardian angel which showed John the heart of that particular church. John saw their faults and their good qualities. I believe that each ministry has a guardian angel appointed over it. It is important to know they are also the recording "secretaries" of all church activity, including observing the handling of all finances.

The Angel of Revelation Five

In Revelation 5:2 we see the scene in Heaven in which

95

a "strong angel" proclaims with a loud voice, *"...Who is worthy to open the book, and to loose the seals thereof?"* (Revelation 5:1)

This is no doubt the great angel who is in charge of keeping all the records in Heaven. It was only proper that he should cry out for the one who was worthy, for that book was full of messages of judgment upon a sinful world.

The Angel over the 144,000 (Revelation 7:1-4)

The numbering of the 144,000 from the tribes of Israel and their marking was under the supervision of an angel who ascended from the east, having the seal of the living God in his authority.

Just before he appears, we see four angels standing in the four corners of the earth, *"holding the four winds of the earth that the wind should not blow on the earth nor on the sea nor on any tree."* They had the power to hurt the earth and the sea.

But the great angel from the east who had the seal of God said to them: *"...Hurt not the earth, neither the sea, nor the trees, till we have sealed the servants of our God in their foreheads."* (Verse 3) This reminds us of Ezekiel 9:6. The great angel from the east will come out of his region and begin his end-time ministry by first sealing in the 12,000 from each of the tribes of Israel. This is the angel that watches over the tribes of Israel and his ministry is to call out the tribes of Israel in the last days and preserve 12,000 from each tribe when the judgment begins.

The First Seven Great Angels of Judgment in Revelation

Seven great angels who are in charge of pouring out the judgments and wrath of God upon the earth are released right after the 144,000 are sealed for protection, the angel at the altar has cast fire, which he took from the heavenly altar, upon the earth (Revelation 8:5).

Let us look briefly at these seven angels of judgment and their part in the end-time punishment upon the inhabitants of the earth. Each one sounds a trumpet before he begins his terrible work of judgment.

1. The First Angel: *"The first angel sounded, and there followed hail and fire mingled with blood, and they were cast upon the earth: and the third part of trees was burnt up, and all green grass was burnt up."* (Revelation 8:7)

Hail and fire mingled with blood was seen falling upon the earth and one third of the trees and of the grass was burnt up.

2. The Second Angel: *"And the second angel sounded, and as it were a great mountain burning with fire was cast into the sea: and the third part of the sea became blood; and the third part of the creatures which were in the sea, and had life, died; and the third part of the ships were destroyed."* (Revelation 8:8, 9)

A third of the seas were turned into blood, and one third of the living creatures, fish, crab, oysters, lobsters, shrimp, prawns, etc. etc. were destroyed. Woe to the seafood lovers!

One third of the ships were destroyed. Fishing industry, navies, both merchant and military will be devastated. The great mountain could be a meteor.

3. The Third Angel: *"And the third angel sounded, and there fell a great star from heaven, burning as it were a lamp,* *and it fell upon the third part of the rivers, and upon the fountains of waters; And the name of the star is called Wormwood: and the third part of the waters became wormwood; and many men died of the waters, because they were made bitter.''* (Revelation 8:10, 11)

One third of all rivers, streams, brooks, inland lakes and waters are destroyed, causing a terrible death to all people who live in the cities that are supplied by the waters that are contaminated by this wormwood poisoning. In Exodus 15:23 we read about the bitter waters of Marah which Moses healed when he obeyed God by casting a tree into the pool so that the people were able to drink and not be poisoned. Wormwood means bitterness. There is a connection between the wormwood of Revelation and the bitterness of Exodus. Both caused death.

4. The Fourth Angel: *"And the fourth angel sounded, and the third part of the sun was smitten, and the third part of the moon, and the third part of the stars; so as the third part of them was darkened, and the day shone not for a third part of it, and the night likewise. And I beheld, and heard an angel flying through the midst of heaven, saying with a loud voice, Woe, woe, woe, to the inhabiters of the earth by reason of the other voices of the trumpet of the three angels, which are yet to sound!"* (Revelation 8:12, 13)

A third part of the sun was smitten, a third part of the moon was smitten and a third part of the stars was smitten. This caused total darkness for a third part of the day and a third part of the night, a darkness which could be felt (Exodus 10:21-29).

Immediately after this terrible darkness, a darkness so terrible it will be felt, an angel of warning flew through the midst of Heaven crying a warning because the sounding of the next three trumpets would cause even greater devastation to the earth.

5. The Fifth Angel (Revelation 9:1-12): When this angel sounded, a star fell from Heaven. This star, which could be another angel or a person, was given a key to the bottomless pit which opened this terrible pit and released smoke like the pillar of a nuclear bomb which again caused darkness. But what was worse: mingled with this smoke were locusts which had scorpion-like power to sting and torment mankind for five months. The only ones over which these terrible demon-like creatures (which were more like demons than animals or insects) had no power, were God's people who still had the mark that the angel had placed on their foreheads.

6. The Sixth Angel (Revelation 9:13-21): *"And the sixth angel sounded, and I heard a voice from the four horns of the golden altar which is before God."* (Revelation 9:13)

The four angels which were bound at the River Euphrates were loosed. They were terrible powerful supernatural beings who had been held back until this year, month, day and hour. Now they were released to fulfill their awful mission. Working with them, under their control were 200 million warriors who killed one third of mankind.

The tragic part is that after this awful plague of death and destruction men still did not repent of their sins. And now time is running out. God gives the world one last warning through the two witnesses of Revelation 11.

7. The Seventh Angel: *"And the seventh angel sounded; and there were great voices in heaven, saying, The kingdoms of this world are become the kingdoms of our Lord, and of his Christ; and he shall reign for ever and ever."* (Revelation 11:15)

This ushers in the final judgment (verses 18 and 19).

Chapter twelve is a review of the scene of the church through all ages until this hour of tribulation times. It is this angel who seals up the church (Revelation 10:7).

The End-Time Angel (Revelation 10:1-6)

"And I saw another mighty angel come down from heaven, clothed with a cloud: and a rainbow was upon his head, and his face was as it were the sun, and his feet as pillars of fire: And he had in his hand a little book open: and he set his right foot upon the sea, and his left foot on the earth, And cried with a loud voice, as when a lion roareth: and when he had cried, seven thunders uttered their voices...And the angel which I saw stand upon the sea and upon the earth lifted up his hand to heaven. And sware by him that liveth for ever and ever, who created heaven, and the things that therein are, and the earth, and the things that therein are, and the sea, and the things which are therein, that there should be time no longer." (Revelation 10:1-3, 5-6)

This is the angel over the end-time ministries. We know this because he says, there should be time no longer. That means "end-time." What is it the end of? It is the end of the days of God's grace, the end of the Church Age, (as the next verse clearly says), the mystery of God (Jesus and His Bride) is finished. Many Bible scholars of prophecy believe this is when the rapture will take place.

Remember, the Book of Revelation is not written in a way that its prophetic fulfillment can be interpeted chronologically.

In the Book of Revelation, different scenes which appear to be happening one after another could be taking place at the same time. That means that things written about in chapters 11-18 could have already taken place during this time of judgment. Whether they have or not, we know all those terrible things which will take place during these days of great tribulation will be supervised by the angels. God will not let anything happen of which He is not in full control.

Because this Bible study is not a Bible study on the Book of Revelation, we will now leave these angels to continue their work of judgment throughout the tribulation period as is described by John so vividly. It would be helpful for you to study the entire Book of Revelation and underline or circle every time it mentions "angel." You will see how God's heavenly host is in full control of every single act of judgment that takes place. The tribulation that we will soon experience (some even believe it has already begun) will be totally under the supervision of God's holy angels. (Even the devil and the anti-Christ can only go so far). These angels are our friends. They have been commissioned to minister to us. They are the ones who will cause the fire of God to fall on the wicked cities. They know who we are. They know our addresses. They see the "scarlet cord" in our windows. We are safe. Whatever comes, we are safe. As long as we are trusting in the shed Blood of the Lamb of God, the destroying angel, as he passes through the land, will see the sign of the Blood and he will pass over us to strike only those who do not have the mark of God on their foreheads. So do not fear any of these things which shall shortly come to pass.

STUDY QUESTIONS

1. Read the Book of Revelation.

2. What happens just before the seven trumpets are sounded?

3. What happens after each of the seven angels sound their trumpets?

4. What is the important thing for us to know concerning the work of these angels in the last days?

5. How can we be secure in face of the coming judgments?

CHAPTER TWELVE

ANGEL STORIES

The following are actual experiences of angelic visitations which people have had. I am including these accounts as they were told to me.

Thirteen at the Table

We have had the privilege of hearing Gladys Triplett give her amazing experience of the angel who came to her home and ministered to the family in a time of great need. Gladys spoke at the End-Time Handmaidens 4th World Convention in 1979 at Dogpatch, Arkansas.

The plainly dressed woman who rang the doorbell at our home in Newberg, Oregon, about 10:30 one morning, was a complete stranger to me. So weak and ill I could scarcely stand, I clung to the door for support. All I grasped from what she said was the word "prayer." Since I assumed she had come for help and my husband was away in another city, sick and dizzy though I was, I felt I should not turn her away.

I invited her in and sank weakly to my knees beside the couch as she removed a damp scarf from her rain-bedraggled hair and laid aside her coat. As I started to ask about her need, she said, "I did not come for prayer. The Father hath sent me to minister unto thee, dear child. He hath sent me to thee because of thy distress and great need. Thou didst call with all thine heart and thou didst ask in faith."

With that, she lifted me in her arms, laid me on the couch, covered me, and said, "When thou didst cry unto Him in the night, thy Heavenly Father heard thy prayer. Sleep now, my child, for He cares for you."

Marveling, I said, "Oh, thank you. But — how did you get here?"

"As the crow flies, came I unto thee," was her strange reply. "Because of the cry of thy heart in thy great need."

She asked if she might use my bathroom to wash and when she returned, she seemed almost a different person. There was no trace of her having been in the rain. Her thick auburn hair appeared freshly combed, with braids coiled softly about her head. There was an indescribable glow on her shining face, though it was a plain, sweet face.

This was the last I remember, for I, who had not been able to sleep for several nights, promptly slept. Only God knows how much I needed it.

We had pastored churches in California, Michigan and Iowa since our marriage, but had only recently come to Oregon, my home state. The pastor of the Assembly of God at Newberg had asked me to help with Sunday school and young people's work and house-to-house visitation, as I was able. My husband was holding meetings in surrounding churches while waiting for a pastorate. When he had been called for this revival, he had hesitated to leave me. My strength had not fully returned after the birth of the new baby-our eighth. However, I did not want to hinder his ministry. I assured him we would manage in some way, as the children had all been taught to work and were good to help me.

On this particular Monday morning, after a sleepless night, I had fallen asleep about the time we should have been getting up and had overslept. We had hurried through a quick breakfast, but took time for our morning devotions. Throughout our married life we have always tried to have Bible reading and prayer with all the children together right after breakfast.

The two oldest children, Loren, a high school freshman, and Delta, our eighth grade daughter, usually did the dishes, but this morning, I had hurried them off to school. Delta, a capable little helper, saw my need and wanted to help, but I thought she should not stay out of school another day. The children always took care of their own rooms and made their beds, but everything was topsy-turvy on this rainy morning because we had been so short of time. We agreed they could all pitch in and help after school.

When the door closed after the last child, I was so exhausted I felt I could not go on through that day. The mountain of dirty dishes, the unmade beds, a cluttered house, and a large laundry overwhelmed me. I collapsed on the couch, hoping to rest enough to gain strength to bathe the two little ones, but had been interrupted by the woman at the door.

Three hours later, when I awoke refreshed, I lay looking in dazed disbelief at my transformed house. All the children's toys and belongings had been picked up, and the floors were clean. My three-month-old baby, freshly bathed, was asleep in her crib. The dining table was extended to full length, spread with my best table service, with places for thirteen-plus the high chair for our sixteen-month-old girl.

The appearance of the kitchen was even more astounding. The heaps of dirty dishes had been washed and put away. The toddler, who usually was not still for a moment, was clean and sitting quietly in a chair by the table, playing with a spoon. **This she had never done!** There was a freshly baked cake, a large bowl of salad, and some other prepared food on the drainboard.

Even **this** was not the most bewildering. The basket of baby laundry and a full hamper of family laundry, plus the bedding from all the beds that had been changed on Saturday, had been washed, dried, ironed, and put away. My guest was just folding the ironing board. I stared in disbelief. My washing machine was certainly not capable of putting out that many loads in three hours. I had no drier, and it was raining. How had she accomplished this? My usual three full baskets of ironing took me parts of two days and often the children helped to finish after school. Yet, she had done it all. I found later that each child's clothing had been folded and put in the proper dresser drawers and that all the beds had been made.

As I expressed my thankfulness and wonder at the transformation of the house, I asked, "*How* could you get so much done in such a short time?"

"It is not by my might, but God's enablements," she said.

I asked where she lived, where she had spent the night, and other questions, trying to find out who she was and where she had come from, but her answers were strange and impossible to comprehend.

Finally, I asked, "Why is all this food prepared and the dining table set? We ordinarily eat in the kitchen when my husband is away and we don't have **that many** in our family."

Her reply left me almost speechless. "Oh, my child, you will be having guests soon."

I gasped. "Thirteen at the table?"

"Yes," she repeated, "thirteen at the table."

We talked in the kitchen for some time. I well remember my strange feeling of awe as she sweetly ministered to me in words of faith. I was absolutely confounded over it all. **I still am**. However, I know her words will never fade from my memory.

As the children came from school, each took a look at my guest and came over near me. I could tell they were puzzled. Several of the younger ones whispered, "Who is she, Mama? She looks funny — kinda different-like."

Earlier, I had asked her name so I might introduce her to my family. She answered, "Just say I am a friend, or a child of God, that came because of your prayer." So I told the children, "This is a wonderful lady that God sent to help me today. You see, Mommie prayed for help through the night, and God sent this wonderful friend."

When my husband returned quite unexpectedly, soon after the children came home, there were five extra persons with him. There had been a death within the church, and the meeting had been closed for a few days. Since my husband had left our car for me to use, the pastor, his wife, their daughter, and another couple had driven over to bring him home. He would return

107

later to continue the meetings.

Our guest was just preparing to leave when Mr. Triplett came into the kitchen. I introduced her to him, as I had to the children. He sweetly said, "That's just wonderful. It's just like Jesus."

At five o'clock, when we were seated around the dinner table, with our six older children, the two of us, and the five guests, there were thirteen at the table — plus the toddler in the high chair and the baby in her crib.

Our guest vanished for a time, and we found all the cooking utensils had been washed.

What could I have done, in my weakened condition, in my untidy house, without the help of this amazing guest? I would have been embarrassed to tears. My husband and family would have been ashamed, for we normally kept our housework done. The guests could not have felt welcome, or at ease. What I might have been able to prepare for them to eat under those conditions, I do not know. Any woman who has been embarrassed by a similar predicament can appreciate my boundless gratitude to God for the help of this marvelous visitor.

We could not comprehend what our eyes had seen. We had never heard of such a visitation. Though we knew it was **utterly impossible** for any human to do all that had been done in such a short time, in our fleshly curiosity and unbelief, we questioned friends, neighbors, even the police in our small town, about the stranger. No one had heard of such a person and no one could give us any clue as to her identity. Our only explanation is that she was a ministering angel *"sent* *forth to minister for them who shall be heirs of salvation."* (Hebrews 1:14)

I have never been able to speak of this experience without being melted to tears at the unspeakable mercy and tender, loving-kindness of my Heavenly Father to send help in my extremity. It has been so sacred, I have not shared it often for fear others might scoff in unbelief. I affirm, as God is my Judge, that this happened, as related. I had dragged through days; prayed through the nights for strength to keep going; and God, who is alive forevermore, answered my prayer.

"O the depth of the riches both of the wisdom and knowledge of God! how unsearchable are his judgments, and his ways past finding out!" (Romans 11:33)

The Invisible Made Visible

My friend, Brother Frans, who has had a special ministry to Christians in the persecuted lands for many years tells the following thrilling encounter with an angel. In this instance he was making a trip into East Germany, and his camper was loaded with clothes, Bibles, cassette players, cassettes and a radio that he was bringing to the Christians in East Germany. After crossing the West German passport control and part of the East German passport and customs control, the following incident happened to Brother Frans:

...A military police sat in his little house. He opened the window and I gave him my passport. He checked my face with the picture in the passport, and asked me, "The second passport please." I said, "What do you mean sir, I have only one passport." The man said, "I need to see the passport of the man who is with

109

you, sir." At this very moment I felt a tremendous power in the cabin of the Volkswagen camper. Again I told the military police, "Sir, I am travelling alone from Holland and I gave you my passport, I think everything is fine." The man raised out of his chair, came out of the little office and stood near me while I sat in my car. "Could you give the passport of the man who sits there next to you, please." In that moment I had such a joy, blessing and power, I could not turn my face and I could not give him an answer either.

It was taking some time and the man said, "Ok, if you do not ask him, I will ask him personally." He walked around the camper and opened the door on the right side, then I turned my face and together we saw — nobody was there.

The military policeman looked into the bus and his face was amazed. I do not know how to describe the feeling between this man and myself. It took some minutes and then the military policeman said, "Sir, are you a believer?"

My answer was, "Yes, sir, I am on the way to visit a church in your country."

Powerfully the military policeman said, "That must have been an angel I saw, I have some faith also. Can you pray for me sometime?" Then he changed his voice and said, "Please not now, go ahead and have a good time."...

Angels Protect Evangelistic Meetings

Aimee Semple McPherson, the great American evangelist, tells how angels undertook when demon-controlled men attempted to destroy an evangelistic meeting:

I drove us toward Philadelphia and the scene of our nationwide camp meeting beginning in July 1917. Saints came from New York, Baltimore, Washington. Hundreds upon hundreds of godly men and women standing upon their feet, hands lifted toward heaven, eyes closed, and upturned faces streaming with tears as they sang the new song of heavenly anthems prompted by the Holy Spirit, provided never-to-be-forgotten sights and sounds. They prayed as I had never heard people pray before. Each one, forgetting his neighbor, forgetting all else but the God who answers prayer, cried out with all his might for a great revival.

Trouble arose upon the second night, however. It developed that the site of our campground had been used by the young men of a neighboring Catholic college for a football field. These young men resented our presence very much and patrolled the grounds day and night, keeping watch on everything and everybody, declaring that we had invaded their own hill, although I had rented it in a regular manner.

While an enormous crowd filled the tent, these young men by the hundreds formed a fringe on the outside. Every time there would be a manifestation of the Spirit, they would burst forth in peals of laughter, ridiculing and mocking. Finally their scoffing and jeering became so loud that it drowned out the voices of any who started to sing solos, lead in prayer, or speak.

The devil had carefully laid his plan. It so happened at this time that a riot took place in the center of the city which had called every available policeman, so there were none to keep order. Back and forth, to and fro, the mob surged on every hand. Detectives told me later that there had been a prearranged program to wipe out every tent on the ground that night, the young men having even gone to the length of concealing cans of kerosene and gasoline behind hammocks of grass that they might later ignite the entire highly inflammable canvas.

Speaking being impossible, the song leader simply directed the audience in the singing of such old songs as "Rock of Ages Cleft for Me," "Nearer My God to Thee," "It is Well with My Soul," and "Jesus, Oh How Sweet the Name." "Oh Lord, I groaned, leaning back in my chair upon the platform, "what shall I do?"

"Begin praising Me out loud," answered the Spirit down deep in my heart, "for the joy of the Lord is your strength."

"But, Lord, how can I praise Thee when I do not feel like it...when I feel like running away?"

"Do you praise Me because you feel like it or because I am worthy?" questioned the Inner Voice.

"Because You are worthy," I answered. "Bless the Lord! Hallelujah! Glory to Jesus!" I began timidly, in a soft voice.

Instantly it was as though strong winds of thanksgiving lifted me above the danger and peril of the moment. My voice became stronger until at last I was truly shouting with my eyes still tightly closed, "Amen! Glory, glory, glory! Praise the Lord, oh, my soul, and all that is within me praise his holy name!"

The congregation caught the Spirit and likewise lifted their voices. As I praised the Lord, I seemed to see a lot of demons with outspread, batlike wings, each of which was interlocked with that of his neighbor, surrounding the tabernacle. But every time I cried "Praise the Lord!" I noted that the demonic forces took a step backward until finally back, back, back, they disappeared amid the trees. But now that I had once begun, it was difficult to stop, so I continued shouting, "Glory to Jesus! Hallelujah! Praise the Lord!"

Suddenly I noticed that from the place where the powers of darkness had been lost to view, a great square of white-robed angels were advancing with outspread wings, each of which likewise was interlocked with that of his neighbor. Bless the Lord! With each "Praise the Lord," the angels took a step forward. On, on, on they came until they entirely surrounded the outer edges of my canvas cathedral.

Startled, I opened my eyes and looked about me. The young men who had been our tormentors were still there, but now they stood as quiet as mice, eyes rounded and staring as they looked upon me wondering-like. Then I arose and preached to one of the most attentive audiences it had ever been my privilege to address. When the altar call was given, the benches were thronged. The same young men, many of whom gave their hearts to Christ, came again and again, bringing the sick and afflicted for prayer. God marvelously answered.

(This is an excerpt from the book *Aimee*, the biography of Aimee Semple McPherson. See the advertisement in the back of this book. This article was used by permission.)

The Hitch-Hiking Angel

Recently there have been many reports of people giving rides to angels on the highways. This has happened, not only in America, but also in Europe. Here is one report we took from the *Billings Gazette*, of July 26, 1980:

Little Rock (UPI) — Reports of a mysterious hitchhiker who talks about the second coming of Jesus Christ, then disappears into thin air from moving cars, has sparked the imaginations of highway travelers and mystified the State Police.

"It sure is a weird story," Trooper Robert Roten said Friday.

Roten said the state police had had two reports — both on a Sunday — that a clean-cut, well-dressed hitchhiker had disappeared from cars traveling along highways near Little Rock.

Efforts to find someone who actually saw the "highway apostle" proved fruitless. But Little Rock apparently is full of people who know someone who knows someone who had it happen to them.

One woman told the story thus:

"The girl said her parents and another couple were coming from Pine Bluff. They picked up this neatly dressed man because he looked like he needed transportation, you know. He discussed current events — he knew about the hostages — and all of a sudden he said, 'Jesus Christ is coming again' and disappeared.

"They stopped the first trooper they saw and told him, 'You're going to think we're crazy' and told him about it. And he said, 'No, you're the fourth party that's told me about it today.' "

"There's not much we can do on a report like that," Roten said. "It's not a violation of the law and no hazard is involved. It's illegal to hitchhike, but if he disappears, this hitchhiker's going to be hard to arrest."

My nephew, David Bergman has had this same kind of experience:

"Be not forgetful to entertain strangers, for thereby some have entertained angels unawares." (Hebrews 13:2)

In the spring of 1982, I was kind to a stranger who happened to be an angel. This is my story.

As an insurance salesman in Arkansas, I was used to driving all over the state to solicit my policies. I had never picked up a rider before or since in my many miles of travelling. It was a Monday morning and I had just left my home office in Harrison, Arkansas. It being the first day of the work week, I was trying to get my enthusiasm and PMA (positive mental attitude) up for the door-to-door canvassing in Marshall. Passing through Western Grove, I saw a hitchhiker on the side of the road. That was it! I would pick him up, be kind to someone and be off to the right start. I pulled into the next drive, turned around to pick up my "attitude adjuster" and he was gone. A car right behind me had picked up my friend. So much for being off to a good start. I was depressed! Reluctantly I got back on the highway to head back to my next town. What could I do? I couldn't go to work like this, down on myself. Just as I was praying what to do next, not one mile down the road from the last hitchhiker was another one. Wow! This could be my day after all! I slammed on the brakes,

115

backed up the car and my "good deed" jumped in. After introducing ourselves, I found out he wanted to go to "the next town." No problem, I'd just sit back and drive.

Right "out of the blue" this guy asks, "Well, David, where do you go to church?" I thought, "Who is this guy? I don't know him from Adam and he's asking me where I attend church." I answered him truthfully, "I am not going regularly anywhere, just bouncing around from Baptist to Assembly of God and don't have my own church."

While I was telling him this sad truth, I thought, "Who is this guy? I have never seen him before and he's asking me personal questions. I'll get even with him, I'll ask him where he goes to church. So I did and he replied, "the Church of St. Paul." I immediately assumed he was a Catholic. Just as if he was reading my thoughts, he said, "where Jesus Christ is the cornerstone." Wow! Totally shocked I drove on quietly to the next town. As I stopped in St. Joe, I shook his hand and he got out of my car. As he walked down the road, I realized what had just happened. I had just entertained my own angel — quite unaware.

My angel was about six feet tall, around 180 pounds and had straight blond hair. He also had the fairest skin I had ever seen. He appeared to be 25 to 30 years of age.

Angels Find Lost Jewellery

Different friends have told me their amazing story of how angels have helped them find jewellery. God cares about the things that are important to us. Perhaps there even are angels who are in charge of the Lost and Found Department!

I changed clothes to work in the yard, and left on my favorite pair of white earrings. Later I returned to the house for a paper towel to wipe the perspiration and noted that the right earring was gone. I had been pushing under shrubbery with that side to get weeds, etc. out. My sister was watering tomato plants to my right, a little distance away. She asked which one was lost, and when I said the right one, she confirmed that it **had** been on in the yard, for she had noticed it. We both looked and couldn't find it. In the house I had said: "Lord, nothing is lost in Your Kingdom, I thank you for helping me find it." But we didn't.

On July 4, when I opened the dresser drawer, I saw the jewelry box where I keep white earrings, open, the lid standing up, and there in the upper left corner, all by itself, was the lost earring! The other one was still on the dresser top where I had put it on returning to the house. I thought my sister, to have some fun, had found it and put it in the jewelry box. So I told her I had caught up with her and had found the earring where she had put it. She **hadn't**. So I said, "Then an angel of the Lord did, for I prayed yesterday and repeated the prayer." She looked unbelieving, but, praise God, this is the only thing that COULD have happened. (Bonnie Harmon, Mississippi)

Angel on Car Hood

One of our End-Time Handmaidens who has been a missionary to Mexico had the following experience:

About two weeks ago, I saw an angel sitting on top of the hood of my car as I was driving home one night.

The angel was pointing upwards with his right arm towards Heaven. In my spirit I knew he was saying, "Keep your eyes on Jesus." The angel appeared for about half a second and was smiling and very, very transparent and fair. (Heather Forrester Elsen, Florida)

Angel in the Back Seat of Automobile

Linda Petersen, the mother of a bright, active four-year-old reports:

Two specific incidents involving angels come to mind with regard to my daughter, Kirstin, the "almost" four year old. Her natural ability to get herself in trouble in one way or another makes me think the Lord has extra angels assigned to care for her. Thus, explaining the frequency with which we note their presence about her.

One morning I was on my way to Bible study (and to drop her off at the central nursery care) for a group of studies in our town. I was late, as usual, so I did not hear immediately what she was saying to me. (She talks constantly, most of the time to hear her own voice, so I just plain ignored her.) About halfway across town it finally dawned on me that she was speaking directly to me and the tone in her voice at this point said, "You better listen to me this time or else!"

"Mother! **Who** are those people in the back seat?!"

People? In the back seat?! I was about to pooh-pooh the whole thing as a three-year old's imagination when I believe the Lord nudged me to consciousness. She REALLY was seeing someone in the back seat of the car and they were God's angels (her guardians?!). As I strained to get a peek in the rear-view mirror and still keep the car on the road, I said to her simply, "They must be the Lord's angels." She immediately settled herself down into the front seat, folded her hands deliberately in her lap and matter-of-factly told me: "Oh, then the nice guy in the middle must be Jesus!"

Jesus!!! Oh, my goodness!!! I completely forgot the fact that I was driving the car and spun around. I saw nothing, but my small daughter assured me they were indeed there, as did the Spirit within me. I am equally confident that they kept the car on the road and that they followed her into the nursery that day and are by her side even now.

Angel Also Protects Kirstin from a Bad Fall

Another precious time occurred when Kirstin was just beginning to toddle about the house on her own. I never knew where she would attempt to go and unlike her older brother she was a "climber."

In our living room we have two matching arm chairs that usually sit with a small table between them. The table is rather unstable and has been upset many times and various glass items shattered. On this particular day this trio was located directly in front of the picture window at the front of the house.

I left my small daughter contentedly playing with her toys on the living room floor while I made a quick trip to the basement. As I came up the stairs and rounded the corner into the kitchen at the very back of the house, I had a full view of the chairs, table and window, but I was some distance from them. I went into a total panic — I couldn't even utter an audible prayer, but the Spirit within me cried out to the Lord. The sight that met my eyes was this:

My curious and trusting child had climbed into one of the chairs with a book to read as I recall. There she had been sitting not **in** the seat, but **on** the arm of the chair with her feet on the seat. My eyes saw her as she stood up and lost her balance and began to fall backward from a standing position over the arm of the chair, onto the table with the glass in front of the glass window.

My body strained as I moved as fast as I could, but it seemed to go nowhere in my panic. I knew there was no possible way for me to reach her before she crashed. But then the whole scene changed right before my eyes! She was not crashing to the floor! There I saw her gently "float" down to the floor as if someone were lifting her and tenderly laying her down. When I did reach her, she lay on the floor **not even near** the dangerous table or the window, but two or three feet **in front of** the chair. She looked up at me, not screaming in fear or tearful and crying, but with a truly angelic smile on her face. As small as she was, she knew the Lord cared for her greatly and so did I! I will praise Him always for that beautiful time for us both to treasure in our hearts. (Linda Petersen, Wisconsin)

Lady Hears Angel Choir

A sister in Christ who was blessed by the "Hallelujah Angel Tape" writes:

I listen to the tape many nights before I sleep. One

reason I am so interested, I heard the angels singing in 1966. The voices were very much like the ones on the tape, only they were singing in tongues and I did not know what they were saying until 1978 when I received the interpretation. They were praising and praising God. (Ethlyn Sayre, New York)

Angel Ministers to Hospital Patient

One time when God sent His angels to personally minister to me, was in October. I was in the hospital and had just had surgery and my gall bladder removed. I was lying in bed in **a lot of pain**, with a friend at my side when the head nurse came into my room and said, "Who was that doctor who was just here?" I looked at my friend and she looked at me, and I told the nurse that there had been no doctor there since early morning. She said that there had just been a tall, dark curly haired doctor at the nurses' station who pulled my chart out of the rack and handed it to her and said, "Go see if she needs something for pain." After the nurse left the room, saying she would bring me something for pain, I looked at my friend and we knew my angel had been at the nurses' desk. Once again God had shown me how very much He loves me. (Sue O'Connor, Ohio)

Angel Comforts Heart-Broken Wife

I was born again on August 25, 1966 on a Thursday morning. Up to this point, we had had a very stormy marriage, as we both had violent tempers and all disagreements, which were many, would end up in screaming, yelling, shouting, obscenities and sometimes physical violence. I had a lot of hate deeply rooted in me and it always came out in our arguments. I never ever kept my peace when David got in a rampage; I would just join him.

Christ so completely changed me the day I was saved, the term "born again" was very fitting. I could hardly believe I was me! I felt such love in my heart, and peace like I'd never known before. I decided to wait till Sunday to tell my husband about my encounter with Jesus. I told him and he said, "That sounds wonderful, but it's hard to believe." Within an hour, at the dinner table he started in on me with his usual criticism and anger. For the first time in our marriage, I didn't respond with anger, but with love and peace in the middle of storm. The angrier he got, the more I smiled at him and the more peace I felt, which made him more angry. The more I smiled in silence, the angrier he got and the more I smiled on and on and on, he got louder and louder, began cursing and yelling; and I just smiled. Finally in sheer exasperation he stood up, pounded his fist on the table and screamed obscenities at me and pointed his finger at my face (this was something I had told him never to do.) When I sat there smiling, he just stared at me in unbelief. I merely said, "Are you through?" He said "yes" and I asked, "May I be excused from the table." He said "yes," and I went to the bathroom and placed my head in my arms as I leaned against the wall, crying my heart out to my newly found Saviour. I wept and wept and wept, until suddenly I heard a noise behind me that sounded like a covey of quail getting up. I quickly turned around and all I saw was a beautiful golden haze — so bright! As I looked directly into it, it vanished, but I knew I had been visited by an angel. (Lucretia Darby, Oklahoma)

Angel Flies with Airliner

On a recent trip by plane from Washington, DC, to Pittsburgh, PA, I was flying alone and sitting behind the left wing next to the window. During take-off I closed my eyes in prayer for all the souls travelling with me and those in control of the flight, ground, air, etc. (this I always do.) I had asked sweet Jesus to send the angels to bear up the plane, thanked Him for doing it, I opened my eyes to see the happiest, laughing angel on the wing looking straight at me. The appearance was brief but it will last a lifetime. What a glorious comfort! (Elizabeth Burdett, South Carolina)

Angel Protects Fearful Woman

One night I was alone and a little afraid in my house. I had asked God to put angels in and around my house. At about 3 a.m. I awakened to see a big angel filling my kitchen. Also I had a sense of several more angels nearby. My fear was gone after that. (Margaret Owsley, Florida)

Child Protected by Angels

When I was a child, I saw angels flying over our hen-house. When I grew up, I lost a sister that I grieved about a lot. I woke up one morning and she was at the foot of my bed. She was dressed in a Grecian gown: white with a cord around the waist. I quit grieving for her, because I knew she was alive. (Lila Welton, California)

Angel Comes to Dinner

In the late thirties we lived in the country and each day my brother and myself would take the cows down the road, to eat the tall green grass that the pastures didn't have any more of since they had eaten it down too short. This gave it a chance to grow again. This one day as we were pasturing the cows by a creek, I noticed a man sitting on the bank of the creek with his dog. He had a staff in his hand, sandals on his feet and a gown on that went down to his ankles. I don't remember who spoke first. But I know I was drawn to him, I had no fear, only a peace. He said, "Would you take me home with you and ask your mother if she would feed me?"

I said, "Sure." We walked together up the road about half a mile: he, his dog and myself. When we got to my house, he sat on the porch. I went in and said to my mother, "I have found a beggar, and he is so hungry. Mother, he wants to know if you will give him something to eat."

My folks had eleven children and those were very hard times. We didn't have much to eat, but Mother never said "no" to anyone. She fixed some eggs and bread and milk to drink. I went out and asked him in. Mother had placed his plate on the long dining room table. It looked so empty, only one plate. When I asked him in, he sat down, folded his hands and, looking up, gave thanks to his Father in Heaven.

I wouldn't leave him. Mother tried to call me into the kitchen, but I wouldn't leave this stranger. I felt drawn to him. Yet I didn't know why. After he ate, he said, "Thank your mother for me." Then he got up and left. I went to the kitchen to tell my mother thank you from the stranger. She went in, picked up his plate and under it was a new $10.00 bill. She said, "Dorothy, run out and catch him and thank him for me." But in only seconds he was gone, his dog with him, too. I looked up and down the road but there was no one.

I have never forgotten this. Many times Mother had said how she prayed for money to buy groceries. There was no work for anyone. We raised our living. So we have always felt Jesus or an angel visited us.

This is only one time; since I was a child I have had many more. Once I was in a car accident. I died, and went before a bright light and heard God's voice. Another time I was put in a morgue, because everyone thought I was dead. But always a power brought me back. God is all powerful. He is all we have to trust in. (Dorothy Greene, Michigan)

Was This an Angel or was it Jesus Himself?

...At the close of the meeting, he (the evangelist) asked everyone to exchange a quick embrace and say, "Jesus loves you and so do I." We were seated in the second row from the front and at the opposite end of the main aisle. As we stood, we greeted everyone in front of us and then my eyes were drawn to the end of our row where a man was standing, "ignoring" everyone else and being "ignored," looking and smiling at me, never taking his eyes off me. I stepped around my friend and walked towards him — the feeling that came over me I can't explain in words! His eyes were so clear and steady I had the feeling he was looking right through me, but they were filled with God's love. I couldn't reach out and embrace him, as I had the others, but could only extend a hand and say, "Jesus loves you and I do, too." He hadn't spoken up to this point but replied, "And I love you."

I stepped out into the aisle, followed by my friend. She neither saw nor spoke to him, as we started down the aisle, in a double line. A wheelchair was blocking one of the lines, so I stopped to let others pass only to look up and see him in the other line, smiling and with a gesture of his hands, letting me go first. Again, no spoken words. I thanked him and we walked out. Again, my friend saw none of this.... (Evelyn Galle)

Angel Drives Car

I had such an experience about ten days ago. My car stalled in an intersection while turning left. I was in the on-coming traffic lane. I had a friend and my two children in the car. I panicked and put my car in "park." A camper-van was coming toward us and seemed oblivious to the fact I was stalled in his lane. I am sure I put my foot on the gas in a last minute attempt to go through the intersection and in the nick of time my car went through and I pulled out to the side of the road. I said to my friend, "How did my car get through the lane when I had it in "park." She is an unbeliever right now, but she said, "There must have been such a force behind the car, that it went through." I know an angel pushed me through, as last week I experimented with my car while in "park" and all the car did was roar the engine and did not move. I put it in neutral and it did nothing at all. I remember going through the lane and hearing a distinct clicking noise like something was taking place against the gears of the car! Praise the Lord! (Kathy Thorne, British Columbia, Canada).

Australian Lady Sees Angel When But a Child

I truly love the angel on your prayer letters, for when I was a little girl out on the farm, one night, I was sitting on the end of my bed, looking out of the window, and I saw a beautiful angel flying across the span of the window. Praise Him! There was God speaking to me way back then when I was a little girl, praise His wonderful Name. (Eva McEachern, Wodonga, Australia)

Angel Stops Scolding Mother with a Smile

Once as I was going to reprimand one of my kids, but I was stopped by a smiling angel who was so tall, I started laughing instead of yelling. (Kaye Raley, Michigan)

Angel Stops Backslidden Wife from Committing Suicide

I am almost 86 now and from the time I was five years old, God has been my Father and Counsellor. At 15 I was converted, at 16 immersed. I had a beautiful experience at that time. The church was filled with the glory of God. When I was thirty, I received the Baptism of the Holy Spirit. After that I loved a man that was far below me spiritually. I got on a detour and I thought I would never get back on the main line again and was going to take my own life, when Archangel Michael came to me, he took the bottle of sleeping pills out of my hand and held them high and just looked at me. He didn't say a word, but he saved my life and I was back on the straight and narrow path very soon, and it really changed my whole life. Up to then I hadn't done much with my life. Later I wrote a book and painted beautiful pictures. I have been tempted many times and always the memory of beloved Prince Michael's eyes shines before me. Now, to all you dear ones who get on the wrong trail, there is always an angel to show you the way back. (Pauline Wattson, New Mexico)

Lady Hears Angel Choir

Dear Sister Gwen, I feel I just have to write you and let you know what a blessing your tape, "Hallelujah Angels" is to me. A dear sister and friend in the Lord, E.F., whom I believe you met through Mary with whom she stayed for a month, played the tape to me. I just cried as I thought I would never hear such singing this side of Heaven again.

Let me explain. Before I was saved I dabbled in

128

the occult, and after my salvation Satan tried many times to get me back. One particular night I had a bad dream. I dreamt I had rejected Jesus and was doing horrible, demonic things and enjoying it. I awoke and felt dirty. I called on Jesus for forgiveness and to give me something in place of that dream. In what I have always thought was another dream, I saw the Heavens roll away. As I looked up, I saw thousands upon thousands of faces and the singing was too beautiful. It was exactly the same singing that is on your tape. That is why I just cried when I heard it as I could see again the choir of angels as in the dream; or it could have been a vision as it was very real. (Lyn Lategan, Republic of South Africa)

Angel Helps Lift Heavy Gate in Place

I, too, have had an exciting experience with an angel. My donkey, Patrick, had lifted a very large corral gate off its hinges and was about to let the two ponies and himself out for a scamper around our neighborhood. I ran down to the gate and tried to lift it, however, I couldn't budge it, as it weighed a couple of hundred pounds. I was pretty new "in the Lord," but ventured out in faith and asked Jesus to send me a holy guardian angel to lift it. He did (although I couldn't see Him) and "we" lifted it onto the hinges with **no** effort on my part! (Barbara M. Lynn)

Child Hears Angel at Christmas

Dear Sister Gwen, when I read your June issue of

your sharing letter, you mention that there is a miracle tape of angels singing. It brought tears to my eyes because the Lord permitted me to hear angels sing around Christmas time when I was a child and in 1975 when visiting a prophet of the Lord. It is too beautiful to describe... (Johanna von Trapp, Washington)

Johanna is the sixth child of the famous von Trapp singing family from Austria whose story was filmed in "The Sound of Music."

Gabriel Escorts Airliner from St. Louis to Miami

My dear Cuban friend Isabel shared with our prayer group. She had been to visit relatives in Miami. Flying back to St. Louis, a "beig-beig" (big) angel appeared on the wing of the plane. "He was 'veery' strong and tall and had on an armor." He would appear and disappear all the way home. She is just recently Spirit-filled and she pondered all this — a few days later, while watching 700 Club, Helen Schneider, who sculptures angels, was the guest. She showed the very one Isabel had seen. It was Gabriel. Pray for her. Her husband is a doctor. (Helen Leckrone, Illinois)

Angels Protect Sleeping Child

I had only been a Christian about two months when I decided that it was time I put my daughter, then about two years old, in her own room in a bed by herself. I had always had her in a crib in our room, but as I was expecting a second child, I needed the crib and knew also that she was too old to be in the room with

Mommy and Daddy. When I first put her in her own room, she cried every night and often fell out of the bed. This was very upsetting to me and I was troubled about it, but did not know exactly how to handle the situation. The only thing I could do, of course, was go to the Father. That night when I put Niki in her bed, I knelt down to pray with her and for her and as the Spirit gave me utterance, I heard myself say, "Father, I give the angels charge over this loved one to protect her and keep her from falling out of bed." I got up to walk away, and the Lord bade me to turn around and look, and I saw two beautiful angels bending down right where I had been, very deep in conversation and watching over my little girl! I walked away with a deep "knowing" that my problem was solved by the Lord God and never again was I troubled over it and Niki never fell out of bed again and never again cried to come to bed with Mommy and Daddy! This is the incident that taught me to pray for the ministering angels to minister to the heirs of salvation and praise God, I have been using this key ever since. (Sandy Long, Tennessee)

Angel Stands by Through Very Difficult Times

I am a very plain person and work outside of my home at an office job. I have a husband and three sons. Several years ago I was sitting at my dining room table, reading my Bible when God spoke to me very clearly in an audible voice and said, "This is God speaking, don't be afraid, you will have angels with you." I was not afraid and told my husband about it. He was outside at the time. It was in the wintertime. Snow was on the

131

ground and he was pulling the boys and having fun with them on their sled. Following this were a series of terrible happenings in my life of which I won't go into detail right now. But one night, as I was sleeping, I was pleasantly awakened and felt prompted to turn to my left side and as I turned over in my bed, I saw the most beautiful angel anyone could imagine. I first noticed the beautiful, very white wings that were perfect. There were layers upon layers of well-matched feathers, so lovely. As I looked up into the angel's face, the angel spoke to me and said, "Hello." I answered by saying, "hello." Then I very peacefully turned over to go back to sleep, but after thinking over what had actually happened, I got a little frightened and turned back to see the angel again and the angel was gone. The angel was very large and seemed to me almost touched the ceiling. But I will never forget the beautiful expression and the love that came from the angel's face. It was God's love. It was so wonderful and beautiful I can't put it in words. (Fran McCollister)

Angels Protect Home

One hot summer morning, around 6 a.m., when all my windows and shades were up, I was feeding my daughter of a couple of months, when there came a pounding at my door. When I went to see what the commotion was all about, I found a policeman telling me that he had just chased a "Peeping Tom" from my kitchen window. Needless to say, I was rather shaken, since I live alone with my daughter. Later that day, I called my spiritual leader, and she prayed that Jesus would send His angels to protect me.

That night, I awoke after dreaming that there was an angel sitting in each chair in my living room, all with clubs in their hands. I laughed to myself about the dream, thinking that this was the silliest dream I had ever had, but I couldn't get over the enormous peace that had come over me. So I laughed and thought, "Well, if there are angels in the living room, I'm being protected," and I went to sleep!

The next day I told my spiritual leader about my dream, and she said, "Thank you Jesus! Pam, do you know what happened? Susie and I prayed last night that Jesus would reveal His angels to you in some way to let you know that you were protected, so that you would have peace!" I was slightly astounded and very, very pleased. (Pam Price, Missouri)

Angel Plays with End-Time Handmaiden's Baby

In 1968, in the early morning, I was suddenly awakened. All was still. It seemed that I could even hear the stillness. I knew I was going to see something. I fact, a lady that lived on the third floor had been to my apartment in the early part of the evening and she had told me that I was going to have a visitor, but would not tell me what or who it would be. All the lights were out. Andre, my son, was about eight or nine months old. He used to run around and around the sides of his baby bed, reaching and laughing at something which I could not see, making coo-coo sounds as he played. I always felt strange when he did this.

Suddenly that night, the angel appeared between

133

my bed and Andre's baby bed. He protruded through the wall from his waist upwards, the rest of his body being on the other side of the wall. I could not see the rest of him, but I was given to know that he was wearing a long, glowing gown that extended to his feet. I could see through his wings, they were like transparent crystal — most beautiful! The wings extended out from both sides of his back. They were spread open the whole time he was there in my bedroom. He had long, golden hair.

He never spoke nor made a sound, but turned his head slowly, looking at Andre, then at me and again at Andre and then at me. His body was about three feet from the floor. It was a sight to see an angel protruding through the wall! Then suddenly he was gone. He just disappeared. (Darlene Brown, Missouri)

Angels Protect from Great Danger

Three black men came to my car and were dragging me out to rob or even kill me. I cried out, "Jesus!" A tall man in white appeared and the three men fled. I turned to thank him, but he was not there. I know it was an angel of the Lord. (Robert Smith, Georgia)

A Testimony from the Far East Broadcasting Company (a Christian Radio Ministry in the Orient)

Come with me to a coastal city of China. It is the midnight hour...plus thirty minutes. A weary little Chinese mother sleeps soundly, exhausted by the anxiety and concern she has had for her son, who labours in a distant government mining operation. At exactly the hour of 12:30 A.M., she suddenly awakens. In moments she arouses the rest of her household to tell them of a dream she has just had: "Two angelic beings came to me in my dream. With them was my son. My son was clothed in a white gown. He comforted me and asked me not to feel bad for him. He told me that he was now back in his heavenly home. As I awoke and turned on the light, my son and the two angels disappeared!" Her family, all unbelievers, laughed at her and said her story was nonsense. With the following sunrise, the secretary from the government mine came to her door. Before he could say anything, she told him that she already knew why he had come: "There was an accident at the mine...at exactly 12:30 this morning," she said. With amazement the mine secretary replied, "The Time was exactly 12:30. The mine collapsed...and your son is dead." The Chinese mother was puzzled. **Her son was not a Christian!** How could he be in the heavenly home? What did the midnight dream mean? Not until she went to the mine to collect her son's belongings. Her son, she learned, had come to faith in Christ beside his little radio! Apparently, he had been listening to a Gospel broadcast over F.E.B.C.

Angel Comes to Take Little Child Home

When little Katherine was five years old, she became very ill with the measles and then whooping cough. When the doctor told Katherine's mother that the little girl was dying and very weak, Mrs. Wright knelt beside her bed and wept. Little Katherine said, "Oh, Mama, don't cry, the beautiful angel is here. See? He's taking care of me." Shortly after this visitation Katherine was escorted home to glory. (Carolyn Wright, Tennessee)

Angel Joins in Worship with End-Time Handmaidens and Servants in Chapel at Engeltal

A few years ago, during our morning devotions at Engeltal, God was taking us through a period of very high worship and praise, reaching into the realm of prophecy. On two of these mornings, two of the girls felt the floor move and heard someone walk into the chapel. They opened their eyes and saw no one! We discussed it later and felt that either the Lord or one of His angels had joined the high praises with us.

The third morning, we again heard the footsteps and the floor creak and felt a strange anointing come into the chapel. The worship took on even a deeper intensity as our visitor joined us. Suddenly, the Lord opened my eyes to see "her." I say "her" because I can only describe what I saw according to my human understanding and this angel was very beautiful and feminine looking. I knew that she had come from the presence of God. As she stood in the centre of the chapel, she had her hands raised up to the throne room, worshipping God.

I was frozen to the spot as I stood in awe of her purity and her single-mindedness as she fixed her eyes upon the Father. Her eyes had depths to them which I have never seen in any human. They were so fastened upon God that she was absorbing his very presence and character! That is true worship!! I have never forgotten this sight and it has influenced my own worship as I seek to have the presence of God within myself.

Let me describe this angel as I saw her. She wore a long, flowing gown of a type of gold, very light material, almost gossimer. It seemed to have neither weight nor substance and sparkled with the glory of God. Around her waist she wore a white belt, bordered with gold and written on it in letters of gold were the words "King of Kings and Lord of Lords." The belt was worn as a sash, crossing over on the right side and trailing down her gown. Her hair was very thick with flowing gold waves and curls. It was taken up at the sides and held back with two sparkling golden barretts. It flowed down to her waist. Her face was indescribably beautiful and flawless, but as soon as my eyes went to her face, they were immediately drawn into the depths of those clear eyes. She had very powerful and large wings, which gave such a feeling of comfort and strength. The feathers of those wings were soft, yet strong and lay neatly in place one upon the other. They looked just like feathers as we know them, but had no spine or quill in the centre.

It is a picture which has never left me. I remember, too, the holiness of God which her presence exuded. It is no wonder that we fear, we cannot stand in the face of such holiness. When I asked God why He had sent her, He said, "I have sent her to teach you to worship!" Praise God! What a lot we have to learn from the angels. (O. T. S., Engeltal)

137

Angel Warns of Shortness of Time

In the summer of 1981 during the month of August I was working in Bethlehem, down in the basement. During this time I was going through some important changes in my life, both spiritual and emotional, which were for the good. I was beginning to find out how much I was really worth to God and how important I am, as we all are, to Him. I had a poor self-image and a defeatist attitude but my encounter changed all that.

I had been pulling some electrical wire through the studs in the wall, thinking the whole time that I wasn't worth anything to anybody or even to God spiritually, but all I was good for was work. As I was working, I felt the presence of a supernatural being. As I looked up, a figure of a man of about seven feet tall filled the doorway. There were no features, but he had a heavenly glow that would only be described as the brightest flourescent light you could ever look at. The other man in the room did not see the angel but felt his presence. I have never felt such power in my life. I felt such love that could not be described, such peace and joy. I could hardly stand before this being, it was so powerful. The appearance only lasted about ten seconds, but it seemed like hours. The angel spoke two things to me. One was to work very quickly, time is very short. There was such emphasis on the shortness of time, and surely we can all feel we are in the last hours of the last days. The second was a word for me from the Lord God which was and still is personal. All that I can say is I found my worth to God that day. People have asked me how do I know it was not Jesus that appeared to me that day, and my answer to that is, I didn't fall before him and worship him. Surely this was a ministering messenger angel sent from God. For the rest of that day I was so overwhelmed with the power of God I couldn't work or hardly function. The appearance and message was a temporary thing, but the effects have been permanent. (Randy Smith, Rainbow House, Niagara Falls, New York)

Angels Accompany the Presence of God

I have come to the conclusion of this Bible study with some of the beautiful testimonies of eye witness accounts from friends and acquaintances who have been ministered to by angels. I know that even though we do not see them, they always are round about us. They bring the presence of God to us. In closing, I want to share one more experience with you which is so beautifully portrayed by our dear friend, the artist Jim Wright, on the cover of this book.

In 1970, I lived alone in a small studio apartment in Chicago. I had come to a crisis time in my life. In desperation I began a lengthy water fast. At the conclusion of the fast, I was suddenly awakened one night by the Presence of God. I opened my eyes to see a great host of angels descending from Heaven. They descended in a ray of golden glory in circular spiral movement until they dropped into my room, but there were so many that the train of angels went all the way from my room up, up, into the sky as far as I could see.

God spoke to me, "You have been waiting for me to speak to you. I am here now. Sit up and write. I am going to talk to you now."

In the light of the presence of God (I did not see God)

and His angels, I wrote many pages as He answered many questions I had in my heart. The glory of God is often accompanied by angels. They bring the sweet presence of God with them.

I pray that this Bible Study may have been a blessing and a comfort to you. If you have had a precious experience with angels, please write and share it with me. I would love to hear about it.

As the days of darkness draw nigh, my prayer for you is that God will send His angels to watch over you and your loved ones for they have a commission from the Father to minister to all those who are heirs of salvation (Hebrews 1:14).

Adam and Eve are sent out of the Garden of Eden (Genesis 3:23, 24).

Jacob wrestles with the Angel of the Lord at Peniel (Genesis 33:24-32).

The Passover (Exodus 12:23).

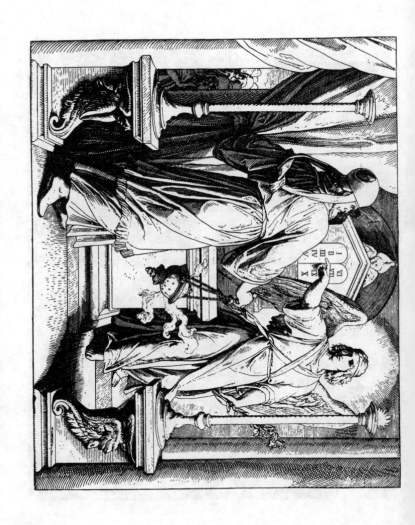

Gabriel visits Zacharias in the Temple (Luke 1:5-20).

"Fear not! I bring you good tidings of great joy." (Luke 2:8-15)

"He is not here...He is risen!" (Luke 24:6)

More Life-Changing Books

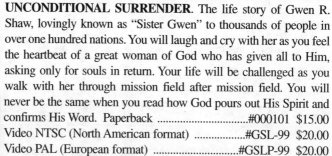

IN THE BEGINNING — *A daily devotional based on the book of Genesis.* The Book of Genesis is perhaps the most important book in the Old Testament. It is the foundation stone of all knowledge and wisdom. Deep and wonderful truths hidden in the pages of Genesis are revealed in this devotional book. You'll be amazed at the soul-stirring writings inspired by the well-known stories of Genesis. Hardcover .... #000211 $27.95

DEEPEN YOUR WALK WITH GOD WITH CLASSIC ANOINTED BIBLE STUDIES BY GWEN SHAW!

BEHOLD THE BRIDEGROOM COMETH! A Bible study on the soon return of Jesus Christ. With so many false teachings these days, it is important that we realize how imminent the rapture of the saints of God really is ....#000304 $6.50

ENDUED WITH LIGHT TO REIGN FOREVER. This deeply profound Bible study reveals the characteristics of the eternal, supernatural, creative light of God as found in His Word. The "Father of Lights," created man in His image. He longs for man to step out of darkness and into His light ....#000306 $5.00

GOD'S END-TIME BATTLE-PLAN. This study on spiritual warfare gives you the biblical weapons for spiritual warfare such as victory through dancing, shouting, praising, uplifted hands, marching, etc. It has been a great help to many who have been bound by tradition. ....#000305 $8.00

IT'S TIME FOR REVIVAL. A Bible study on revival that not only gives scriptural promises of the end-time revival, but also presents the stories of revivals in the past and the revivalists whom God used. It will stir your heart and encourage you to believe for great revival! ....#000311 $7.75

OUR MINISTERING ANGELS. A scriptural Bible study on the topic of angels. Angels will be playing a more and more prominent part in these last days. We need to understand about them and their ministry. Read exciting accounts of angelic help ....#000308 $7.50

POUR OUT YOUR HEART. A wonderful Bible study on travailing prayer. The hour has come to intercede before the throne of God. The call to intercession is for everyone, and we must carry the Lord's burden and weep for the lost so that the harvest can be brought in quickly...#000301 $5.00

REDEEMING THE LAND. A Bible study on spiritual warfare. This important teaching will help you know your authority through the Blood of Jesus to dislodge evil spirits, break the curse, and restore God's blessing upon the land. ....#000309 $9.50

THE FINE LINE. This Bible study clearly magnifies the "fine line" of difference between the soul realm and the spirit realm. Both are intangible and therefore cannot be discerned with the five senses, but must be discerned by the Holy Spirit and the Word of God. A must for the deeper Christian...#000307 $6.00

THE POWER OF THE PRECIOUS BLOOD. A Bible study on the Blood of Jesus. The author shares how it was revealed to her how much Satan fears Jesus' Blood. This Bible study will help you overcome and destroy the works of Satan in your life and the lives of loved ones!
....#000303 $5.00

THE POWER OF PRAISE. When God created the heavens and the earth, He was surrounded by praise. Miracles happen when holy people praise a Holy God! Praise is the language of creation. If prayer can move the hand of God, how much more praise can move Him!
....#000312 $5.00

YE SHALL RECEIVE POWER FROM ON HIGH. This is a much needed foundational teaching on the Baptism of the Holy Spirit. It will enable you to teach this subject, as well as to understand these truths more fully yourself ....#000310 $5.00

YOUR APPOINTMENT WITH GOD. A Bible study on fasting. Fasting is one of the most neglected sources of power over bondages of Satan that God has given the Church. The author's experiences shared in this Bible study will change your life ....#000302 $5.00

4

The Women of the Bible Series by Gwen Shaw,

opens a window into the lives of the women of the Bible in the style of historical novels. Their joys and heartaches were the same as ours today.

EVE—MOTHER OF US ALL. Read the life story of the first woman. Discover the secrets of one of the most neglected and misunderstood stories in history ....#000801 $4.50

SARAH—PRINCESS OF ALL MANKIND. She was beautiful — and barren. Feel the heartbeat and struggles of this woman who left so great an impact on us all..#000802 $4.50

REBEKAH—THE BRIDE. The destiny of the world was determined when she said three simple words, "I will go!" Enjoy this touching story. ....#000803 $4.50

LEAH AND RACHEL—THE TWIN WIVES OF JACOB. You will feel their dreams, their pains, their jealousies and their love for one man. ....#000804 $4.50

MIRIAM—THE PROPHETESS. Miriam was the first female to lead worship, the first woman to whom the Lord gave the title "Leader of God's people."..#000805 $7.50

Other Books by Gwen Shaw

GOING HOME. This book is a treasure which answers so many questions and comforts so many hearts. It gives strength and faith, and helps one to cope with the pain of the loss of a loved one. This book is not really a book about dying, but about Going Home to our Eternal Abode with our loving Heavenly Father......................#000607 $8.00

LOVE, THE LAW OF THE ANGELS. This is undoubtedly the greatest of Gwen Shaw's writings. It carries a message of healing and life in a sad and fallen civilization. Love heals the broken-hearted and sets disarray in order. You will never be the same after reading this beautiful book about love. ....#000601 $10.00

SONG OF LOVE. She was a heart-broken missionary, far from home. She cried out to God for help. He spoke, "Turn to the Song of Solomon and read!" As she turned in obedience, the Lord took her into the "Throne Room" of Heaven and taught her about the love of Christ for His Bride, the church. She fell in love with Jesus afresh, and you will too ....#000401 $7.50

5

THE FALSE FAST. Now, from the pen of Gwen Shaw, author of Your Appointment With God (a Bible Study on fasting), comes an exposé on the False Fast. It will help you to examine your motives for fasting, and make your foundations sure, so that your fast will be a potent tool in the hands of God......................................#000602 $2.50

THE LIGHT WILL COME FROM RUSSIA. The thrilling testimony of Mother Barbara, Abbess of the Mount of Olives in Jerusalem. She shares prophecies which were given to her concerning the nations of the world in our time by a holy bishop of the Kremlin, ten days before his death just prior to the Russian Revolution ....#000606 $5.50

THE PARABLE OF THE GOLDEN RAIN. This is the story of how revivals come and go, and a true picture, in parable language, of how the Church tries to replace the genuine move of the Spirit with man-made programs and tactics. It's amusing and convicting at the same time ....#000603 $4.00

THEY SHALL MOUNT UP WITH WINGS AS EAGLES. Though you may feel old or tired, if you wait on the Lord, you shall mount up on wings as eagles! Let this book encourage you to stretch your wings and fulfill your destiny — no matter what your age! ....#000604 $6.95

TO BE LIKE JESUS. Based on her Throne Room experience in 1971, the author shares the Father's heart about our place as sons in His Family. Nothing is more important than To Be Like Jesus! ....#000605 $6.95

POCKET SERMON BOOKS BY GWEN SHAW

BEHOLD, THIS DREAMER COMETH. Dreams and dreamers are God's gift to humanity to bring His purposes into the hearts of mankind. The life of Joseph, the dreamer, will encourage you to believe God to fulfill the dream He has put into your heart......................#000707 $2.00

BREAKTHROUGH. Just like when Peter was in prison, sometimes you need a "breakthrough" in your life! This book reveals the truth in a fresh and living way! ....#000708 $2.00

DON'T STRIKE THE ROCK! When Moses became angry with the people's rebellion and disobeyed God's order to speak to the Rock, it cost him his entrance into the Promised Land. Don't allow anything to keep you from fulfilling God's perfect will for your life!..........#000704 $2.00

6

GOD WILL DESTROY THE VEIL OF BLINDNESS. "...as the veil of the Temple was rent...I shall again rend the veil in two....for...the Arab, so they shall know that I am God...." This was the word of the Lord concerning God's plan for the nations in the days to come. Join in with Abraham's prayer "Let Ishmael live before Thee!"................#000712 $2.00

HASTENING OUR REDEMPTION. All of Heaven and Earth are waiting for the Body of Christ to rise up in maturity and reclaim what we lost in the Fall of Man. Applying the Blood of Jesus is the key to *Hastening Our Redemption* ....#000705 $1.50

 IT CAN BE AVERTED. Many people today are burdened and fearful over prophecies of doom and destruction. However, the Bible is clear that God prefers mercy over judgment when His people humble themselves and pray..#000706 $2.00

KAIROS TIME. That once in a lifetime opportunity—that second, or minute, or hour, or year, or even longer, when a golden opportunity is sovereignly given to us by the Almighty. What we do with it can change our lives and possibly even change the world...................#000709 $1.50

 KNOWING ONE ANOTHER IN THE SPIRIT. Experience great peace as you learn to understand the difficulties your friends, enemies and loved ones face that help to form their character. "Wherefore henceforth know we no man after the flesh..." (II Cor. 5:16a) ....#000703 $2.00

THE ANOINTING BREAKS THE YOKE. Learn how the anointing of God can set you free from your bondage: free to fulfill your destiny in the call of God on your life!...#000710 $1.50

 THE CRUCIFIED LIFE. When you suffer, knowing the cause is not your own sin, for you have searched your heart before God, then you must accept that it is God doing a new thing in your life. Let joy rise up within you because you are a partaker of Christ's suffering ....#000701 $2.00

THE MASTER IS COME AND CALLETH FOR THEE. Read about how the Lord called Gwen Shaw to begin the ministry of the End-Time Handmaidens and Servants. Perhaps the Master is also calling you into His service. Bring Him the fragments of your life — He will put them together again. An anointed message booklet ....#000702 $1.50

 THE MERCY SEAT. The Days of Grace are coming to a close, and the Days of Mercy are now here. And oh, how we need mercy! There never has been a time when we needed it more!................#000711 $2.00

8